HUNTER
FROM THE
HEART
LAND

HUNTER FROM THE HEART LAND

RECIPES & STORIES FROM MASTERCHEF FAVOURITE

CAMERON PETLEY

Food photography by Kieran Scott

RANDOM HOUSE
NEW ZEALAND

A RANDOM HOUSE BOOK
published by Random House New Zealand

18 Poland Road, Glenfield, Auckland, New Zealand

For more information about our titles
go to www.randomhouse.co.nz

A catalogue record for this book is available
from the National Library of New Zealand

Random House New Zealand is part of the Random
House Group

New York   London   Sydney   Auckland
Delhi   Johannesburg

First published 2012
© 2012 text and recipes Cameron Petley; photography
Kieran Scott

The moral rights of the author have been asserted

ISBN 978 1 86979 825 3

Design: areadesign.co.nz

Printed in China by Everbest Printing Co Ltd

For my Pop (Awhe)

CONTENTS

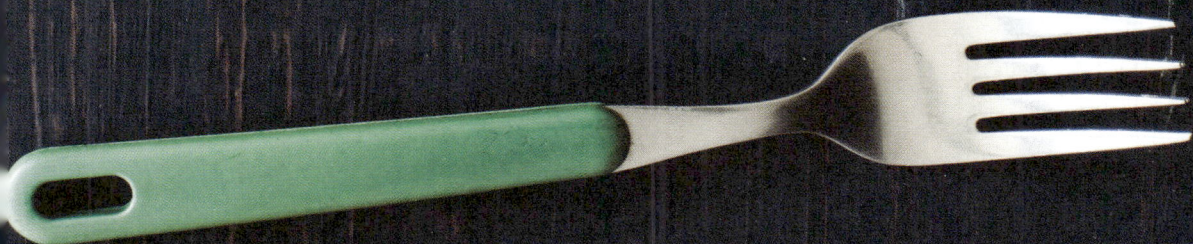

INTRODUCTION

I've been really into food since I was a little kid. I grew up in Tokoroa but my mum's from Waiohau at the bottom of Te Urewera, and we spent all our holidays at our grandparents' farm down there with my uncles and aunts and cousins. Mum's brothers taught me the ropes of the hunter-gatherer life from a really young age.

My grandparents lived way out in the middle of nowhere where there was no supermarket or anything, so it was a matter of having to get our own food. We had to or we'd get really hungry!

One of the good things about learning to find our own food was that it was all about spending time with the family and passing knowledge down through the generations — and it still is. My uncles started us off catching eels and trout in the Rangitāiki River. As soon as I learned to catch these foods, my uncles taught me how to clean them up, which was sliming the eels and gutting the fish, and then how to cook them.

So we started off with the little stuff like catching eels and trout in the river, and getting pipis and cockles at the beach. When we got older, we got more into hunting. We'd jump on the horses and head into the bush, going after deer or pigs. It was always a buzz to spend time hunting with my cousins and to be able to put meat on the table for the family. We'd get whatever wild things we could. Going out and getting food was just what we did. We didn't have video games and all that stuff then. I was brought up to get out there in nature, and I reckon it was a great way to grow up.

My parents both worked busy jobs at Kinleith in Tokoroa. When they were working, my Auntie Violet used to look after us. She was a good cook. Sometimes, after she'd spent the morning cooking us up a big feast, she'd get us out of school for lunch. Me, my brother Leif and my cousin Eru loved it. We'd have a big feed like boil-ups, roasts, corned silverside — real farmer meals — then there'd always be rice pudding or bread pudding, and after eating all that we wouldn't want to go back to school. Auntie Violet used to have to ring my dad and he'd come over to take us back to school. I think I learned a lot of things from her about cooking too. She'd use bugger-all ingredients but she always knew how to get the most flavour out of things. It's a Māori thing, I think, using bugger all to achieve something tasty.

Even from a really young age, while I was sitting there eating whatever had been cooked up for us, I'd always be thinking, How can I make it taste better?

That's just always how I've been. Not many kids are like that — they only want to eat and be done with it. But I was always trying to think how to make anything we ate taste better.

My mum was a bit of an experimenter when it came to food and my folks would take us out to restaurants quite a bit when we were younger. Not all my friends got to do stuff like that, but Mum was really into food. I remember being taken to an Italian restaurant in Tokoroa and thinking the guy there was the coolest dude in the world because he was cooking all this food and singing away. He just seemed so happy. I thought, I wouldn't mind doing that when I get older. I've always wanted to cook for a living but I didn't really see how it could happen. My wife, Jerusha, and I had kids young so I was always working to look after them — working at the meat works, with both sheep and cattle, and then at the chicken farm. This wasn't really the way I wanted to be working with food, but I learned a lot from my time in those places.

When the opportunity came up to be on *MasterChef*, I thought I'd give it a go. Before that I had never cooked with fancy stuff. I just cooked really simple food that I could mostly go out and get myself. That's still the way I cook. But now I get to cook for other people for a living as Head Chef at The Master's Table. It's what I've always wanted to do. I love that I can serve up wild game and different types of seafood in the restaurant. For me, it's what I've eaten my whole life but it's great to be able to share my way of cooking with other people.

VEN

VENISON

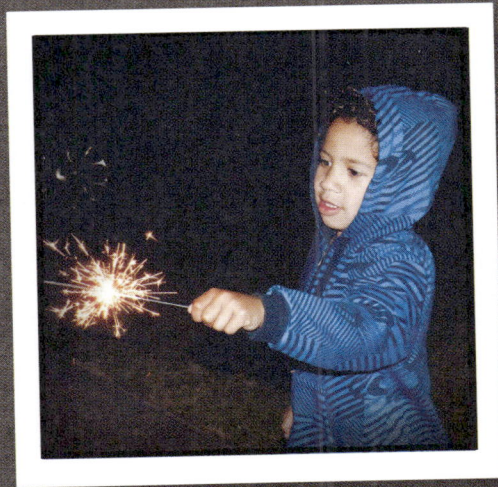

Part of the reason we were taught to find food in the traditional ways was so that when our grandparents and our parents got too old to go hunting themselves, we could do it for them. I want to teach the younger generation so that when I get too old, they'll provide the food for us. Handing down that knowledge is really important to me.

18

During the school holidays in Waiohau, when I was a really little kid, I used to hate having to stay at home with all the girls. I was one of the youngest and I resented watching the older boys doing all the man stuff — eeling, fishing and hunting.

When I got old enough and was allowed to go hunting too, I was stoked. It didn't matter what age you were, as long as you could walk long distances on your own, you were in. There was no way in hell anyone was going to carry you!

At around age 12, my uncles taught us how to use guns. The guns were handed down through the generations. When the uncles knew that we were responsible enough to use a gun, then they would hand them on to us. But they really made sure that we knew what we were doing and we had to prove to them we knew how to use the guns properly before we were allowed to go out shooting.

When we were old enough, my cousins and I would go into Te Urewera on horseback and hunt for deer. We'd just jump on the horses and head into the bush. We didn't take any supplies. We'd just go. We never planned to go for long but we didn't worry too much if we ended up out there for a while. Sometimes we'd just take a wrong turn and get a bit lost so it'd take us a while longer to get out. If we were still out there when it got dark, we'd set up camp and stay put until it got light again. We'd wake up in the morning and be away again. We were never worried.

There are a series of streams — the Mangamako, the Tawhia, the Waihua, the Waikōkopu — off the Rangitāiki River. All of them go up into Te Urewera, so my uncles used to tell us, 'If you ever get lost up there, just find one of the streams and follow it all the way out.' That's what we'd do, and we never got lost.

When we were out in the bush, we knew we'd always be able to find food. Sometimes I'd take a bit of tinfoil with some butter and an onion or something, just in case.

Then if we got stuck out there, I could pull an eel out of the stream. After cleaning and gutting it, I'd fill the eel with chopped onion, cover it in butter and wrap it in the tinfoil. Then I'd just chuck the parcel on the embers and that was dinner. It was delicious.

Back then there were plenty of wild deer so it wasn't often that we'd come back without one. When we got a deer, we'd gut it as quickly as we could so the guts didn't taint the meat. This was important, because it could sometimes be quite a long ride out of the bush. We'd then put the carcass on the back of the horse and carry it home. Those were some of the best times of my life, when we had no plans and could just go with the flow. Doing stuff like that made us young fellas feel more like men.

I used to go deer hunting all the time but it's all about the pigs now. That's because I can't take my dogs with me when I go deer hunting. The dogs are all about trying to make their master happy. If you shoot a possum, they'll think that's what you want and then spend time going after possums. If you shoot a deer, all they'll start looking for is deer. If they're chasing deer, the dogs will end up 10 or 15 kilometres away — that's a long way for me to go and find them. So when I'm out with the dogs, it's strictly pigs that I go after. If I was hunting without the dogs, I'd happily shoot a deer if I came across one, but I don't really ever go hunting without the dogs anymore.

A lot of people are scared of cooking venison. When I went into the *MasterChef* auditions, one of the other contestants asked me what I was cooking. I said, 'Venison.' He was like, 'Ohhh, I don't know about that. No one who cooks venison makes it through.' That got me a bit worried. But I knew I had the right flavours for the meat.

I prefer cooking wild venison over the farmed stuff. The farmed deer spend all their time eating grass so the meat tastes a bit like beef. With the wild deer, they're eating a much more varied diet and you can tell because the flavour is way more intense. It can be too intense for some people but I reckon if you put the right flavours with it to balance out the gaminess, then anyone would like it.

When I'm cooking venison, I do try to think about what the deer would be eating in the wild, as what an animal eats has such an effect on the flavour of the meat.

VENISON BACK STRAP ON SMASHED PURPLE POTATOES WITH RASPBERRY GLAZE

When I cook wild venison I like to use berries to add sweetness to balance the strong flavour of the meat. The vinegar also helps cut through the gaminess and the smashed potatoes make a great accompaniment. When searing meat it's impotant to work quickly using a very hot pan before the oil or butter burns — if it does burn, clean the pan and start again.

Preheat oven to 180°C.

For the venison, season venison well with salt and pepper and rub with oil. Sear in a hot ovenproof frying pan for 2 minutes on each side. Transfer to oven for 10-12 minutes until cooked to medium. Take out and rest for 10 minutes. Slice into about 10 pieces.

For the potatoes, cook potatoes in boiling water until just tender. Cool under cold water to stop further cooking and set aside. Sauté onion and garlic in 25ml of olive oil in a hot frying pan until soft. Smash boiled potatoes with a fork, trying not to mash them, then add to the pan along with rosemary and thyme. Season well and drizzle over remaining olive oil. Stir through and set aside, keeping warm.

For the glaze, place jam and vinegar in a saucepan over a medium heat and reduce, stirring from time to time. Once thickened slightly, add butter and stir through. Then add raspberries and set aside.

To serve, place potatoes in the middle of plates and top with slices of venison. Spoon over glaze and garnish with pea shoots, if desired.

SERVES 2

Venison
1 × 400g venison back strap
salt and pepper
25ml oil
pea shoots for garnish, if desired

Smashed Purple Potatoes
8 small purple potatoes, washed
1 red onion, finely sliced
2 cloves garlic, finely chopped
75ml olive oil
2 sprigs rosemary, finely chopped
1 sprig thyme, finely chopped

Raspberry Glaze
2 tablespoons raspberry jam
4 tablespoons sherry vinegar
15g butter
12 raspberries

VENISON CARPACCIO WITH VEGETABLE SALSA & HORSE-RADISH MAYO

The trick to this recipe is to crush the peppercorns in a pestle and mortar, but not too finely. Serve everything chilled on a cold plate for a cool summer starter.

Roll venison in peppercorns and season well with salt. Roll tightly in cling film and chill for 2 hours.

Place salsa ingredients in a bowl and combine well. Set aside. Combine mayo and horseradish well and set aside.

Remove venison from cling film and thinly slice.

Arrange venison on a platter, spoon over vegetable salsa, drizzle with horseradish mayo and garnish with pea shoots.

SERVES 2

Venison Carpaccio
1 × 200g venison tenderloin
8 tablespoons black peppercorns, crushed
2 tablespoons pink peppercorns, crushed
salt
pea shoots for garnish

Vegetable Salsa
2 radish bulbs, finely diced
1 small red onion, finely diced
1 cucumber, de-seeded and finely diced
100ml white balsamic vinegar
2 tablespoons white sugar
½ teaspoon salt
½ teaspoon pepper

Horseradish Mayo
¼ cup mayo
2 tablespoons horseradish

VENISON CASSEROLE

You can use any cut of meat for this recipe. Cooking the tougher cuts will take longer, but keep checking from time to time so the meat is just how you want it.

Preheat oven to 120°C.

In a cast-iron frying pan or flameproof casserole, brown venison in batches in oil over a medium-hot heat. Remove from pan and set aside.

Brown onion, garlic, carrot and bacon in the same dish. Then return venison to the dish and add bay leaf, thyme, beer and stock. De-glaze the pan, scraping up all those little bits of meat and veg stuck to the bottom. Add tomato purée, balsamic and brown sugar and combine well. Season with salt and pepper. Transfer to an oven dish if using the frying pan and place in oven, covered, for 3 hours or until sauce is thick and meat tender.

Serve with your favourite winter veg and slices of Māori bread (see page 180) with butter.

SERVES 6

1kg venison, cut into large cubes
cooking oil for frying
2 onions, roughly chopped
2 cloves garlic, finely chopped
1 carrot, roughly chopped
200g streaky bacon,
    roughly chopped
1 bay leaf
2 sprigs thyme
1 × 330ml bottle Speight's Old Dark
250ml game stock (see page 172)
2 tablespoons tomato purée
2 tablespoons balsamic vinegar
2 tablespoons brown sugar
salt and pepper

2 EEL

I was probably about five or six when I first got to go out eeling and fishing with my grandfather and uncles. When we were older and we knew what we were doing, me and my cousins would go out fishing or eeling every night.

When my grandfather was growing up, he didn't
have fish hooks or torches or anything like that
— nothing — so he used to lift the rocks out of
the way, put his hands down into the eel holes
and pull the eels out with his hands. As a little
kid, I wasn't too keen to try that.

Those things have got such sharp teeth that if one got you,
you'd know about it.

My other grandfather taught my cousins and me the traditional
methods of catching eels. He took us down to the stream and
showed us how to bob for eels. We would get long, thin strips
of flax and rough them up with the edge of a mussel shell.
The flax would then get tied to a stick. Next we'd go and collect
a whole lot of worms. These weren't just ordinary garden
worms; the worms over where we're from are about 30 or
40 centimetres long — they're really big buggers. After my
cousins and I had gathered up a whole lot of these big worms,
my grandfather would thread the flax through the whole
length of each worm. He'd keep on threading the worms until
he ended up with a couple of metres of flax strung with
worms. That length of flax would then be rolled up into a
ball that we called a 'bob'. It looked pretty gross but the eels
absolutely loved it.

The bob would then get tied to a stick and dangled in the water,
and the eels would go for the worms. Eels' teeth are angled
backwards so once they bite into something, it's really hard for
them to let go. When they bit into the worms, their teeth would
get caught on the roughed-up flax. Once there were enough
eels on the bob, we'd pick up the stick it was attached to and
flick the whole thing out of the water onto the riverbank. Then
we'd hit the eels on the head, slime them, gut them and cook
them up. Beautiful.

Bobbing was one of the first ways I was taught to catch eels
and I've never seen it done quite like this anywhere else.
I remember one time my grandfather left the bob in the

water for so long that it became absolutely smothered in eels. When he went to flick the bob out of the water, it was so heavy and the eels were moving around so much that he ended up getting pulled into the river.

It takes a hell of a lot of eels to pull a fully grown man into a river.

The other way I learned to catch eels was with a baited hīnaki, or fish trap. My cousins and I would go hunting to shoot rabbits to use for bait.

Rabbits were one of the few things that we hunted but never ate. It's kind of funny to think of that now when people are paying top dollar to eat rabbit in restaurants.

Back then, eels were plentiful. Now, some of the streams and rivers have been overfished. You can still find some spots where there are heaps but that's not as easy as it used to be. Not long ago I set a hīnaki in a stream just out of Putaruru and got 17 in there all at once. It was a pretty good haul but you need to know where to go to get decent catches these days.

SMOKED EEL SALAD WITH HORSE-RADISH DRESSING

For the dressing, place jam in a bowl and pop in the microwave for 15 seconds to soften. Add mustard and horseradish and stir through. Then add olive oil and balsamic and combine.

For the salad, place rocket and sliced onion in another bowl. Drizzle dressing over salad, reserving some, and toss through. Arrange on a plate, placing eel slivers on top of salad. Drizzle over remaining dressing and season with salt and pepper. Serve with a squeeze of lemon.

SERVES 2

Horseradish Dressing
2 tablespoons apricot jam
1 tablespoon wholegrain mustard
1 tablespoon grated or
    minced horseradish
25ml olive oil
25ml white balsamic vinegar

Smoked Eel Salad
50g rocket
1 small red onion, sliced
200g smoked eel, thinly sliced
    into horizontal slivers
salt and pepper
1 lemon

POACHED EEL WITH CORIANDER DUMPLINGS

I first got the idea to use smaller-sized eels for this dish from a guy from Mangamuka up north — he told me they work better because they are sweeter and not as fatty. I cook my eel with the skin on and bone in but it works without these too.

For the eel, sweat down onion and garlic in a little oil in a saucepan over a medium heat. Season with salt and pepper and add diced carrot and potatoes. Sprinkle over curry powder and cook for 2 minutes. Add fish stock and eel and poach on a low simmer for 5 minutes.

For the dumplings, combine flour and baking powder in a bowl. Add egg and stir through. Season well with salt and pepper and add chopped coriander. Gradually add water and combine well to form a dough. Roll into approximately a dozen little balls. Place in stock and cook for 10 minutes.

Ladle into bowls and serve garnished with parsley.

SERVES 4

Poached Eel
1 onion, finely chopped
1 clove garlic, finely chopped
cooking oil for frying
salt and pepper
1 carrot, peeled and diced
2 potatoes, peeled and diced
2 tablespoons curry powder
500ml fish stock
1 small eel, cleaned and
   sliced lengthways
chopped parsley for garnish,
   if desired

Coriander Dumplings
1 cup flour
1 tablespoon baking powder
1 egg
salt and pepper
1 bunch coriander, finely chopped
100ml water

SMOKED EEL PIE WITH CREAMY CAULIFLOWER TOPPING

SERVES 2

Creamy Cauliflower Topping
1 head cauliflower, roughly chopped
1 small onion, finely chopped
1 clove garlic, finely chopped
50g butter
50ml cream
salt and pepper
1 tablespoon grated Parmesan
1 teaspoon paprika

Filling
1 leek, finely sliced
1 carrot, peeled and grated
olive oil for frying
50g butter
2 tablespoons flour
200ml milk
300g smoked eel, flaked
1 bunch chives, finely chopped
salt and pepper

For the topping, cook cauliflower in boiling salted water until tender. Drain off excess water and set aside.

Sweat down onion and garlic in a frying pan in a little butter until translucent. Then add cauliflower, remaining butter and cream. Season with salt and pepper. Transfer to a blender and blend to a purée. Set aside.

For the filling, cook leek and carrot in a frying pan over a medium heat in a little olive oil. Set aside.

Melt butter in a saucepan. Add flour and stir continuously until flour cooks through, about 2 minutes. Gradually add milk, stirring continuously until all milk has been added and sauce has thickened. Add cooked leek and carrot, flaked eel and chives and combine. Season with salt and pepper and set aside to cool.

Preheat oven to 180°C.

Spoon eel mixture into two ramekins, leaving 1cm at the top of the dish. Place cauliflower mixture into a piping bag and pipe on top of filling. Lightly dust with Parmesan and paprika and pop in oven for 10–15 minutes.

SHE
FIS

Even though we lived on the farm, we'd quite often drive out to the Bay of Plenty coast — anywhere from Thornton along to Whakatāne, then around to Ōhope and Ōhiwa. Once we got there, we'd go and get a feed of seafood. I loved digging for pipis and cockles. Our uncles also taught us how to get oysters and mussels off the rocks. At Ōhope we used to get horse mussels. I wasn't too keen on those as a kid; they had such a strong flavour and they were almost impossible to eat because they were so big. But it didn't stop me.

I remember when I was about five, going down to Mount Maunganui with my uncle Joe. He'd take his T-shirt off and give it to me to hold. Then he'd swim out into the ocean. He'd go quite a long way out — a couple of hundred metres maybe. I remember thinking the first time he did it, Where the heck is he going? I was a bit worried but it turned out he was swimming to a big rock that was under the water. You would never have known it was there — but he knew. He'd come back in with a big armful of mussels which he'd just drop on the beach. We'd crack the shells together, pull out the mussels and start eating.

With the pipis and the cockles, we'd take a billy — a tin can with a bit of wire over the top — and put it on a fire. We'd chuck some seawater into the billy, throw the shellfish in there and cook it up.

The flavour of the sea in fresh seafood straight from the ocean is more intense than what you get from anything else. It's the real taste of the sea and I love it.

I only got into diving during the last eight or ten years. Now I go diving down the East Coast and get stuff like crayfish, pāua and kina. They're all things I've always really enjoyed eating but in the last few years I've been able to get them myself. Like all food, I reckon it always tastes better if you've gone and got it yourself!

If pāua is cooked badly, people can be completely turned off eating it — especially if it's the first time they've tried it. It's so important to cook it right; a lot of people really overcook pāua and it's just horrible. My wife never ate pāua. She just absolutely refused to because the one time she'd had it, it was overcooked and tough. About eight years ago, I cooked her some creamed pāua (see page 57) and had to almost force her to eat it. It took a while but eventually she gave in. And she loved it. Now, whenever I cook pāua, I have to beat her to it. In fact, I have to race the whole family. Sometimes I wish I'd never convinced them to try it because then there'd be more for me!

Kina is another thing that people seem to have trouble with. I'm quite happy to just eat it plain. I love its pure flavour of the ocean and its sweet creamy texture. But I enjoy trying to come up with ways to cook it that will make people want to eat it. If you just slap kina on a plate, people who haven't tried it before will look at it and think, Ewww. Most of my family wouldn't normally eat kina but when I cook it for them in an omelette (see page 59), they love it. I know I've cooked kina right when people who have previously hated it will happily eat it. You can cook it so it just adds a nice saltiness to the dish without being too dominating.

A lot of traditional Māori recipes came about because people needed ways to keep food for long periods of time. They didn't have fridges so they'd use whatever methods they could to make things last. Meat would be hung up and dried. After a while, the meat would be so dry the flies couldn't penetrate it, so the maggots would be scraped off and you could eat what was underneath. They also used to ferment quite a lot of food. One of those recipes is toroī, which is a fermented mussel dish (see page 49).

When I first tried it, the toroī had been fermenting for nine months. When I took the lid off, the pressure released was huge. It was kind of fizzy and the smell could have stripped paint off the walls. I was trying to dig the mussels out of the jar with a fork but they were that rotten they slipped through the prongs of the fork. I had to get a spoon. I know people who just love that stuff, but I only eat it fresh now.

I like using traditional Māori recipes but putting a spin on them to make them more appealing. Our food culture has such a long history that it's great to bring it to a broader audience.

There's not a lot you can do to some of the dishes but most of them you can change a bit. And some you don't want to change at all. Pork and watercress is such a classic combination. After you've caught a pig, and you've got it home and cleaned it up, you're straight down to the creek to get the watercress. They're perfect together.

Boil-up is another traditional recipe. It's very similar to a French broth or stock. The French boil bones and vegetables in a pot for flavour and don't add much to it. It's all about bringing out the natural flavours of the ingredients. The only difference is the French drain off all the stock and throw the rest away, whereas Māori eat it all.

MARINATED MUSSELS

Always use fresh mussels for this dish and when cleaning them remove the beards plus any stowaways such as crabs. If raw mussels aren't for you, try steaming them open and chilling them beforehand.

Strain off excess moisture from mussels and place them in a bowl. Add red onion, cucumber, tomatoes, sugar, balsamic and parsley and combine well. Season with salt and pepper. Cover and marinate in the fridge for 1 hour.

Serve as a chilled summer side dish at a hāngī or barbecue.

SERVES 2 as an entrée

24 mussels, shelled, de-bearded
    and finely chopped
½ red onion, finely diced
½ cucumber, de-seeded
    and finely diced
2 tomatoes, de-seeded
    and finely diced
4 tablespoons sugar
100ml balsamic vinegar
¼ cup curly-leaf parsley,
    finely chopped
salt and pepper

MARINATED PĀUA

Serve as a side dish at a summer barbecue, or with some steamed veg or Asian greens.

Place all ingredients in a bowl and combine well. Cover and marinate in the fridge for 2 hours.

Place pāua and marinade in a hot frying pan with oil and fry for 5–7 minutes, turning from time to time.

Serve hot as a side dish.

SERVES 4 as an entrée or side dish

300g pāua, cut into thick strips
1 clove garlic, finely sliced
1 red chilli, finely sliced
¼ red onion, finely diced
1 tablespoon red pepper
    finely diced
4 tablespoons chopped coriander
2 tablespoons brown sugar
1 tablespoon fish sauce
2 tablespoons soy sauce
salt and pepper
cooking oil for frying

WATER-CRESS TOROĪ

SERVES 4

2 bunches watercress, cleaned
  and large stalks removed
1 onion, finely chopped
24 mussels, shells cleaned
  and de-bearded
salt

Back in the old days, and even now, Māori tended to let their toroī ferment for up to eight months before eating it, but for me fresh is always the best.

Cook watercress in boiling salted water for 30 minutes. Drain and squeeze out any excess liquid. Finely chop and place in a bowl. Set aside.

Place onions and 2 cups of water in a saucepan. Bring to the boil and once boiling, add mussels. Remove mussels as the shells open. When all mussels are cooked, reserve cooking liquid.

Remove mussel meat from shells and finely chop. Add chopped mussels to watercress. Strain cooking liquid through a sieve and pour over just enough to cover watercress and mussels. Season with salt and refrigerate.

Served chilled. You can store this in the fridge for a few weeks.

MUSSEL FRITTERS WITH CURRY MAYO

For the fritters, place flour, baking powder, onion, garlic, egg, thyme and parsley in a bowl and season well with salt and pepper. Gradually add milk and mix to a thick batter that will hold its shape when cooked. Drain off any excess liquid from mussels, add meat to batter and combine well.

Heat a frying pan to medium and add a knob of butter and a little oil. Ladle in fritter batter, a quarter cup at a time. Cook for 3–4 minutes until fritter is nice and golden brown on the bottom and bubbles appear on the top. Then turn over and cook the other side until cooked through. Drain on paper towels to absorb any excess fat. Keep warm. Repeat with remaining mixture. This makes about 10 fritters.

For the curry mayo, place all ingredients in a bowl and combine well.

Place curry mayo in a dish and serve with mussel fritters.

SERVES 4

Mussel Fritters
1 cup flour
2 teaspoons baking powder
1 small onion, finely chopped
1 clove garlic, finely chopped
1 egg
2 sprigs thyme
4 tablespoons finely
  chopped parsley
salt and pepper
200ml milk
4 cups raw mussel meat,
  roughly chopped
butter and cooking oil for frying

Curry Mayo
¼ cup mayo
2 tablespoons curry powder
½ small red onion, finely diced
2 tablespoons finely
  chopped chives

CRAYFISH & CORN FRITTERS WITH TOMATO SALSA

Try adding finely chopped cooked bacon to the batter to add a smoky flavour. For a full meal, serve with a crispy garden salad.

For the fritters, place flour, eggs and milk in a bowl and combine to make a thick batter. Add spring onion and corn and combine. Then fold in crayfish meat and lemon pepper, and season with salt and pepper.

Heat a frying pan to medium and add a little butter and oil. Spoon fritter mixture into little heaps in pan. Cook each side for 3–4 minutes until brown. Drain on paper towels and keep warm. Repeat with remaining mixture. This makes about 10 fritters.

For the salsa, place chilli, tomatoes, onion, parsley and red pepper in a bowl and combine. Add vinegar and season well with salt and pepper.

Serve fritters with salsa on the side.

SERVES 4

Crayfish and Corn Fritters
6 tablespoons self-raising flour
2 eggs, beaten
¼ cup milk
1 spring onion, finely sliced
½ cup corn kernels
250g cooked cray tails,
    meat cut into 1cm cubes
½ tablespoon lemon pepper
salt and pepper
butter and cooking oil for frying

Tomato Salsa
1 chilli, finely chopped
6 cherry tomatoes, quartered
1 small red onion, finely chopped
2 tablespoons finely
    chopped parsley
1 red pepper, de-seeded
    and finely chopped
2 tablespoons sherry vinegar
salt and pepper

MUSSEL CHOWDER

This recipe is great for those cold days or at the bach because it's so quick and easy. Try adding chilli to turn up the heat.

Bring water to the boil in a saucepan and add mussels, thyme and bay leaf. Steam mussels, removing them as their shells open. When all mussels have opened, strain and reserve stock.

Sweat down onion, garlic and carrot in a saucepan over a medium heat with a little oil. Sprinkle over curry powder and stir. Add reserved stock and reduce by half. Then add cream and reduce until thick. Make a slurry with cornflour and milk and use this to thicken chowder to desired consistency, stirring constantly as you pour it in.

Cut mussels into thirds, place in soup and heat through. Season with salt and pepper. Squeeze over lemon juice and sprinkle with chopped parsley.

Serve in bowls with toasted ciabatta.

SERVES 4

200ml water
24 mussels, shells cleaned
   and de-bearded
2 sprigs thyme
1 bay leaf
1 onion, finely chopped
1 clove garlic, finely chopped
1 carrot, peeled and grated
cooking oil for frying
2 tablespoons curry powder
250ml cream
2 tablespoons cornflour
¼ cup milk
salt and pepper
1 lemon
3 tablespoons chopped parsley
8 slices ciabatta, toasted,
   to serve

CREAMY PĀUA ON TOAST

This was one of my favourite dishes growing up and is a hit among Māori families throughout New Zealand. If you undercook pāua it's going to be tough, if you overcook pāua it's going to be tough. So it's a matter of getting it just right — I like to flash-fry for best results.

Brown onion and garlic in half the butter in a frying pan for 2 minutes. Set aside.

Melt remaining butter in another frying pan and gently fry pāua for 4 minutes until tender. Add cooked onion and garlic and then cream. Stir through and reduce sauce by half or until thickened. Season with salt just before serving.

Serve on toasted ciabatta.

SERVES 2

1 large onion, finely chopped
2 cloves garlic, finely chopped
50g butter
4 pāua, tenderised and
    finely sliced into slivers
100ml cream
salt
2 slices ciabatta, toasted,
    to serve

KINA OMELETTE WITH LEMON SAUCE

This is a good way to introduce people to eating kina. A lot of people who don't usually like kina love it this way. A winning combination of salty, sweet, creamy and crunchy.

For the sauce, place cream and half the kina in a bowl and blend with a stick blender. Add a squeeze of lemon juice and chives, and season with salt and pepper. Blend until slightly thickened.

For the omelette, place beaten egg, remaining kina and cream in a bowl and season well with salt and pepper. Stir to combine, trying not to break up the kina. Set aside.

Melt butter in a hot frying pan and pour in egg and kina mixture. Cook for a few seconds until edges go frilly, then tilt the pan and draw the cooked egg into the centre, letting the uncooked egg run to the outside of the pan. Do this a few more times until omelette is just cooked but still soft in the centre. It is now ready to fold. Fold omelette in half and keep warm.

Wilt down spinach with butter in a hot frying pan and season with salt and pepper.

Place toasted ciabatta on a plate and top with spinach and then omelette. Drizzle over sauce and serve.

SERVES 1

Lemon Sauce
100ml cream
1 × 200g pot of kina
1 lemon
2 tablespoons chopped chives
salt and pepper

Kina Omelette
1 egg, beaten
50ml cream
salt and pepper
25g butter

To Serve
50g baby spinach
25g butter
salt and pepper
1 slice ciabatta, toasted

PĀUA MINI BURGERS

Instead of using egg to bind the ingredients, you can use the hua (intestines) from the pāua's guts, which also adds extra flavour.

Sweat down onion and garlic in a little oil in a frying pan over a medium heat until translucent. Season with salt and pepper and cool.

Place pāua, bacon and egg in a bowl and combine well, Add cooled onion and garlic to pāua and bacon mixture, sprinkle in the flour and combine well.

Shape into six even-sized balls and gently press down to form patties. Lightly dust in flour.

Brown patties in a hot frying pan with a little butter for 2 minutes on each side until cooked.

Assemble burgers — bun base, mayo, salad, pāua patty, tomato sauce, bun top — and serve.

MAKES 6 BURGERS

Pāua Patties
1 onion, finely chopped
2 cloves garlic, finely chopped
cooking oil for frying
salt and pepper
300g minced pāua
6 rashers bacon, finely chopped
1 egg
3 tablespoons self-raising flour
extra flour for dusting
butter for frying

To Assemble
6 mini burger buns, toasted
6 tablespoons mayo
50g salad greens
6 tablespoons tomato sauce

MUSSELS IN ANCHOVY BUTTER

A quick and easy way to serve mussels that will impress the guests. Serve this dish as a starter to get the tastebuds going.

SERVES 2 as an entrée

200ml water
12 mussels, shells cleaned
    and de-bearded
50g butter
6 anchovy fillets
juice of 1 lemon
½ bunch parsley, finely chopped
½ cup breadcrumbs,
    freshly toasted
lemon wedges to serve

Bring water to the boil in a saucepan. Place mussels in pan and steam until shells open. Remove opened mussels from pan and take mussel meat out of the shells. (Reserve cooking liquid for another use.) Set mussel meat aside and clean and reserve shells.

Place butter in a frying pan over medium heat. Add anchovy fillets, mashing them into butter with the back of a spoon. Add lemon juice and stir through. Add mussels to the pan, coating them in butter.

Spoon mussels along with butter into cleaned shells. Combine parsley and toasted breadcrumbs, and sprinkle over mussels.

Serve immediately with lemon wedges.

4 FISH

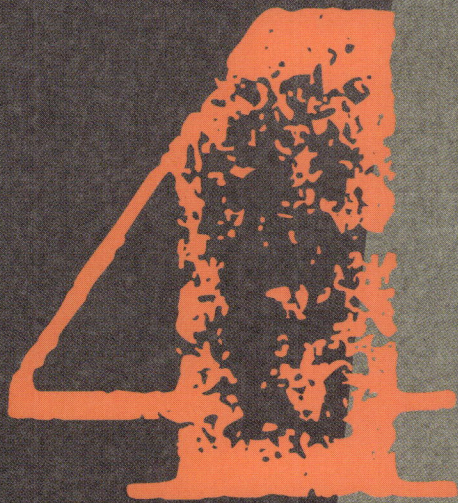

My most memorable fishing trip was on a charter out to the Ranfurly Banks, on the continental shelf about 20 kilometres off East Cape. Before I did that trip I was just a trout fisherman but it totally got me into sea fishing. I went out with Cascade Charters from Whakatāne and it took us about 14 hours to get to the Banks. These charters are so popular you sometimes have to book three years in advance, and some fortunate ones are able to book the same time every year.

Luckily for me, a guy I knew had pulled out and I got to go instead of him. There were six of us on board a 32 foot boat. For some of the journey, we were sailing through 3 to 5 metre swells. It was the first time I'd been on a boat like that so it was a bit scary. I was expecting to be sick, so it was a relief not to be.

The trip was worth it once we got there — a once-in-a-lifetime opportunity.

We were out at sea for four days: the skipper would park up in a shallow bay each night and then in the morning we'd head back into deeper water. It was pretty weird not seeing any land for four days. There are no little fish in the ocean so we caught nice big hāpuka, bass and kingfish. Because the Banks are in the middle of nowhere, there's plenty of fish. When the skipper pulled in to shallow spots, we dived for kina and crayfish as well. It was awesome.

The limit for hāpuka is five a day and we got that easily. It was pretty choice coming back with a good haul of chilled fish.

The hāpuka out there are huge — catching them was like trying to lift up a fridge with a piece of string.

The biggest fish were between 20 and 30 kilograms — I thought they were the hugest fish I'd ever seen but the skipper reckoned they were quite little. I couldn't believe it. Our gear had a 90 kilogram breaking strain so we were never going to get the really big fish. Because the water we were fishing in was so deep, we'd be baiting up the lines with two Puka Bomb sinkers that weighed 340 grams each. Even with two of them, it would take five minutes for the line to hit the seafloor. Then it would take 20 minutes to reel it in — and that's with no fish on the line.

With all that effort, you were praying for a fish to be on the line.

After that trip, I went out a few times from Mount Maunganui and Kāwhia. The difference between fishing off the east coast and fishing off the west coast is massive. Off the Mount, it's always quite calm but even on a good day off Kāwhia, it's pretty choppy. The only time I've been seasick was off Kāwhia! From there, you get good fishing for snapper and gurnard.

My favourite eating fish has to be hāpuka. It's such a nice, meaty, firm-fleshed fish. I love chunky fish that has meaty fillets. I reckon snapper is a bit over-rated but it's a good fighting fish. Snapper will give you a bit of a thrill on the line, whereas hāpuka are kind of a dead weight and don't put up much of a fight.

SALMON STEAKS

SERVES 2

1 × 300g salmon fillet,
  skinned and boned
4 rashers bacon
100g butter
olive oil for frying
2 sprigs thyme

Cut salmon into four strips widthways. Take two strips and turn them on their sides and arrange into half-moon shapes. Interlock half-moons to form a round salmon steak shape, wrap in 2 rashers of bacon and secure with a toothpick. Repeat with remaining salmon and bacon.

Place butter and a splash of olive oil into a frying pan over a medium-hot heat and throw in thyme sprigs. Place steaks in the pan and cook each side for 3–4 minutes, basting continuously. Do not burn butter.

Serve with beetroot and apple chutney (see page 167) and a summer salad.

KINGFISH WITH BROCCOLI & BLUE CHEESE SAUCE

You can use kingfish with the skin on and scaled, but score the skin across the width of the fillet about three centimetres apart to stop the fish curling up when you cook it.

Preheat oven to 180°C.

For the fish, season kingfish fillets with salt and pepper. Gently fry in butter and oil in an ovenproof frying pan for 3-4 minutes. Transfer to preheated oven to cook for a further 5 minutes. Take out and rest for 5 minutes.

For the broccoli and blue cheese sauce, blanch broccoli in hot salted water for 4 minutes then plunge into cooled water to stop any further cooking.

Place crumbled blue cheese and cream in a saucepan over a medium heat and cook until cheese melts and sauce thickens. Season with pepper and squeeze over lemon juice.

Place broccoli into bowls and pour over blue cheese sauce. Serve fish on top.

SERVES 2

Kingfish
2 × 200g kingfish fillets, skinned
salt and pepper
25g butter
cooking oil for frying

Broccoli & Blue Cheese Sauce
300g broccoli
1 wedge blue cheese, crumbled
200ml cream
pepper
1 lemon

WHITEBAIT FRITTERS

When I cook whitebait, I try to not take too much away from its subtle flavour. The best way to enjoy these fritters is smacked between two pieces of bread and butter.

Place egg, flour and lemon pepper in a bowl and combine well. Fold in whitebait.

Heat a little oil and butter in a frying pan over a medium heat. Spoon a heap of whitebait mixture into pan, browning one side. Then, using a fish slice, carefully turn over and cook until golden brown. Repeat with remaining whitebait mixture. This makes 6–8 fritters.

Serve with fresh white bread with lashings of butter.

SERVES 2–4

1 egg, beaten
2 tablespoons flour
1 teaspoon lemon pepper
1 cup whitebait
oil and butter for frying
6–8 slices white bread

HĀPUKA ON HERBED POTATOES WITH CAPER SAUCE

SERVES 2

Herbed Potatoes
3 large potatoes, peeled
olive oil
2 tablespoons chopped rosemary
4 sprigs thyme, leaves only,
   chopped
salt and pepper

Hāpuka
2 × 200g hāpuka fillets, skin on
oil for rubbing and frying
salt and pepper
50g butter

Caper Sauce
200ml cream
4 tablespoons capers
juice of ½ lemon

The salty, tangy caper sauce makes this dish a sure hit. You can use any fresh fish instead of hāpuka.

Preheat oven to 220°C. Line an oven tray with baking paper.

For the potatoes, cut sides off potatoes to get a square or rectangle shape. Then cut into 1cm cubes and wash under running water to remove any starch. Pat dry in a clean cloth.

Toss potato cubes with a splash of olive oil, rosemary, thyme and a generous pinch of salt and pepper. Place on lined oven tray and roast for 15 minutes. Set aside and keep warm.

Decrease oven temperature to 180°C.

For the hāpuka, score skin on fish, rub with oil and season with salt and pepper.

In a medium-hot ovenproof frying pan, cook hāpuka skin side down in butter and oil for 3–4 minutes until skin is crispy. Turn and cook for a further 2 minutes. Transfer to oven and cook for another 4 minutes. Set aside and rest for 5 minutes.

For the sauce, in the same pan used to cook the fish, add cream and capers and bring to the boil. Add lemon juice and reduce until sauce is thick. Keep pan moving so cream doesn't boil over the sides.

Arrange potatoes on plates with fish on top. Drizzle with sauce and serve with your favourite salad.

EASY FISH CURRY WITH BANANAS & PRAWNS

When a workmate introduced me to curry with bananas, I wasn't sold at first. It sounded weird but after trying it, I loved it.

Sweat down onion and garlic in a medium-hot frying pan in a little oil. Add chilli, spring onion and ginger and cook for 2 minutes. Sprinkle over curry powder and cook for another 2 minutes. Then add fish sauce and coconut cream, and bring to the boil.

Turn down the heat to a gentle simmer. Add snapper and poach for 4 minutes. Add prawns and bananas and simmer for another 4 minutes. Add chopped coriander and gently stir through. Season to taste with salt and pepper and a squeeze of lemon juice.

Serve with steamed rice.

SERVES 4

1 onion, sliced
1 clove garlic, finely chopped
cooking oil for frying
1 red chilli, finely chopped
1 spring onion, finely sliced
3cm knob ginger, julienned
2 tablespoons curry powder
1 tablespoon fish sauce
1 × 400ml can coconut cream
2 × 200g snapper fillets, cubed
12 prawns
2 bananas, sliced
1 bunch coriander, finely chopped
salt and pepper
1 lemon

KAHAWAI CROQUETTES

I personally think kahawai is under-rated. I like it because it's oily, firm and chunky — and when it's smoked it's beautiful. Kahawai is great in croquettes; the kids love 'em too.

Place butter in a saucepan over a medium heat. Add flour, stirring continuously until flour cooks through, about 2 minutes. Gradually whisk in milk and cook, stirring, to make a thick and smooth béchamel sauce. Add spring onion, carrot, fish and parsley to the sauce and combine well. Cook for 3 minutes then season with salt and pepper. Remove from heat and cool.

Line a baking tray with baking paper.

Place kahawai mixture in a piping bag and pipe onto the lined baking tray in long, even rows. Cover with cling film and freeze until firm, about 2 hours.

Preheat deep-fryer to 180°C.

Once croquette mixture is firm, cut into pieces 5cm long.

Place flour in a bowl, beaten eggs in another and bread-crumbs in another. Dredge croquettes in flour, then egg mixture and finally coat in breadcrumbs.

Fry in batches in deep-fryer for 6 minutes until golden and crunchy. Drain on paper towels.

Serve with sweet chilli sauce.

SERVES 4

100g butter
6 tablespoons flour
200ml milk
1 spring onion, finely sliced
1 small carrot, peeled and grated
300g smoked kahawai, flaked
½ bunch parsley, finely chopped
salt and pepper
flour for dredging
2 eggs, beaten
2 cups golden breadcrumbs
oil for deep-frying
sweet chilli sauce to serve

RAW FISH

SERVES 4 AS AN ENTRÉE

300g gurnard fillets, cubed
juice of 1½ lemons
150ml coconut cream
100ml cream
1 spring onion, finely chopped
1 small onion, finely chopped
1 carrot, peeled and grated
12 cherry tomatoes, quartered
salt and pepper
lemon wedges to serve

You can use any firm white fish to make this dish, which is a big hit throughout the Pacific. I sometimes use trout fillets but leave out the lemon — either way it's delicious, and remember fresh is always the best. Enjoy.

Place gurnard in a large bowl. Add lemon juice and toss through fish. Leave to marinate until fish flesh takes on a white colour — this should take 5–10 minutes. Drain lemon juice from fish and discard. Add coconut cream, cream, spring onion, onion, carrot and tomatoes and stir thoroughly. Season well with salt and pepper.

Serve with wedges of lemon.

5

TRO

DU'T

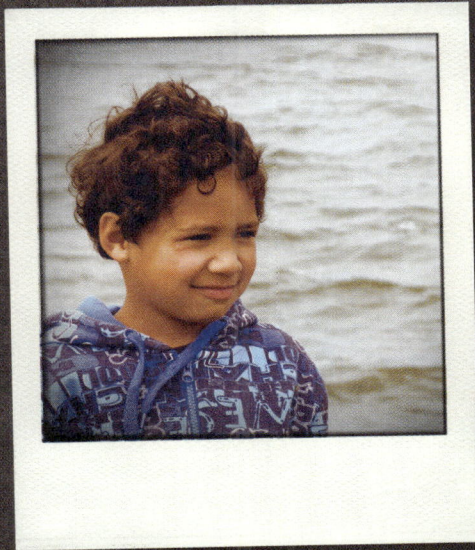

As a kid learning to catch trout, I didn't use a fishing rod. We had streams running through our farm block where the trout would spawn. We used to go down to the stream with a gaff and just spear the fish straight out of the river.

I remember once, when I was about nine or ten, going down to play in the creek with my older cousins. We saw these two trout swimming up the stream and someone called out, 'Oh, look, trout.' As usual we were thinking about getting a feed. I ran back home and grabbed the net. When I got back to the stream, I gave the net to my cousin Casey and he scooped them both up. That was when I first learned that when the trout are spawning, they come up the stream in pairs. After that, every time we fished there during spawning, we knew that if we caught one, there'd be another not too far away.

I know now that fishing like that is completely illegal, but we had no idea back then. It was the way it had always been done. That's how my ancestors caught trout, before there were laws about fishing, and that's how we were taught.

It was good times growing up out there, fishing with my cousins. We were really competitive, always trying to see who could catch the biggest or the most fish.

Trout is a beautiful eating fish and it's good that you can catch them pretty much anywhere. It's a bit of a shame that you can't buy trout, but I guess if it was sold in shops, then people would be cleaning out all the streams and rivers to make a buck. And all the money that gets put into trying to sustain the fishery each year would go to waste.

I'm all about only taking as much as you can eat and I think that's really important when it comes to gathering any wild food.

The trout in the streams where I grew up is different from most of the trout you get around the country. It's quite a pure

wild trout. Most trout around the Waikato and all the way to Taupō feed on kōura, the little freshwater crayfish. Because they're eating crayfish, the trout meat tends to be quite pink — almost like salmon. The trout out of the Rangitāiki River has meat that is almost completely white. It's absolutely delicious eating fish and I especially like it raw, marinated in a bit of coconut cream — kind of like a ceviche but without the lemon juice (see page 82).

PAN-FRIED TROUT WITH ROASTED TOMATOES & PEA & WATER-CRESS PURÉE

SERVES 2

Pea & Watercress Purée
1 cup peas
1 cup watercress
50ml chicken stock
salt and pepper

Roasted Tomatoes
4 vine-ripened Campari tomatoes
50ml balsamic vinegar

Pan-fried Trout
1 × 300g trout fillet, skin on,
  cleaned and boned
salt and pepper
butter and cooking oil for frying
microgreens for garnish

For the purée, cook peas in boiling salted water for 5 minutes, then add watercress and cook for a further 2 minutes. Drain and return vegetables to the saucepan. Add stock and season with salt and pepper. Purée with a stick blender until smooth, and set aside.

Preheat oven to 200°C.

For the tomatoes, place tomatoes on an oven tray. Slice into the top of each tomato in a criss-cross pattern and splash some balsamic into each cut. Season with salt and roast for 10 minutes. Set aside.

For the trout, score trout skin and season with salt and pepper. Fry skin side down for 3 minutes in a little oil and butter in a hot frying pan. Turn and cook for a further 3 minutes.

Serve trout on purée with tomatoes on the side and garnish with microgreens.

TROUT PÂTÉ

MAKES 2 CUPS

200g smoked trout, flaked
zest of 1 lemon
½ cup crème fraîche or quark
1 clove garlic, finely chopped
3 tablespoons finely
** chopped chives**
salt and pepper

If you can't find crème fraîche or quark, cream cheese is fine. Try the pâté with sliced cucumber, a couple of capers and some mayo.

Combine smoked trout, lemon zest, crème fraîche or quark, garlic and chives in a bowl. Season with salt and pepper. Transfer to a mould and refrigerate.

Serve on crackers or crostini.

SMOKED TROUT FETTUCCINE

Cook fettuccine in a saucepan of boiling salted water until al dente (firm to the bite), about 8 minutes. Drain and pour cold water over pasta to stop any further cooking. Drizzle over oil and toss until well coated.

Place pasta in a large frying pan over a medium heat and pour in cream. Spoon pesto over pasta and add fish. When cream starts to bubble, fold pasta through sauce, combining well. When sauce has thickened, season with salt and pepper.

Serve garnished with parsley and sprinkled generously with Parmesan.

SERVES 2

½ 400g packet fettuccine
8 tablespoons olive oil
200ml cream
6 tablespoons pesto
200g smoked trout,
    boned and flaked
salt and pepper
curly-leaf parsley for garnish
2 tablespoons grated
    Parmesan

POBRK

6

Pig hunting is my life now. I'd go all day every day if I could, but my wife won't let me. When I'm in the bush, I just love being there, chasing something around — my heart will be pumping hard out and I get such an adrenalin rush from it that I don't really think of pig hunting as a sport, it's more of an addiction. Most pig hunters have to go hunting or they'll start getting withdrawal symptoms and start losing their minds! I get like that quite a bit. I have to get out there at least once a week to keep sane.

I've been hunting for ages but it wasn't until I had my own dogs that I really got into it. You're not a real pig hunter until you have your own pack. Before I got my dogs, I could only go when my friends felt like it. I finally got my first dog, Girl, off my brother-in-law, Corey, about six years ago after years of thinking about it — and I haven't looked back since. It means that I can go out hunting on my own and I can go whenever and wherever I want. My first dog came with two puppies, Chap and Cole, and since then I've kept adding to the pack.

Taking on dogs is a big commitment when it comes to hunting. They're not pets. The only time they get a really good run around is when you take them out into the bush. You have to make sure you do that pretty often or it's not fair on the dogs.

If you treat your dogs well, they'll stay loyal to you to the very end.

You look after them, they'll look after you — but you've got to put in a lot of hours to get them shaped into the dog you want. I've got seven dogs at the moment and it takes a bit of time and effort to manage the pack. It's important to get the right combination of animals otherwise hunting with them doesn't work.

I like getting my dogs when they're just born or little pups. That way I know how they've been treated their whole lives. I know that they've been looked after and cared for properly. Some dogs are naturals and some take a bit more work but I don't believe there's such a thing as a bad dog — that's just the owner not training their dog properly.

One of the best dogs I have is an absolute natural. Chap was only nine months old when he caught a massive pig all on his own and held it while I came to find him. I was hunting with him and his mum. She took off in one direction after a pig and

Chap turned around and ran back the other way. I thought he'd seen the pig and got scared — I really thought he was running away. I was calling him but he wouldn't come. As he ran off about 300 metres in the opposite direction to where his mum had gone, I was thinking, You stupid mutt . . . Then I heard a bit of a yap and a squeal. I couldn't believe it. The pup caught a pig!

I ran down to where he was and, sure enough, he was hanging on to this huge pig. Before that he'd only ever been on two little pigs but Chap really knew what he was doing. It was pretty funny watching the mum, who'd missed the pig she was after, come running back to help the wee guy out with his catch.

It just proved to me that sometimes you don't have to put any work at all into a dog. Sometimes they just know what to do.

I was rapt that night. That was easily the most memorable pig I've ever caught.

Around Tokoroa and Putaruru, there are plenty of pigs but, like anywhere, you have to know where to find them. That said, this area is also one of the hardest places to catch a pig because there are so many keen hunters around — the Tokoroa pig-hunting club has several thousand members and is the biggest in the country. The pigs here have been dogged since the day they were born so as soon as they hear a truck or a dog panting, they'll take off. To get pigs in an area like this, you need really good dogs. If you get out into the more remote places, the pigs don't run away. They don't even know what a dog is and have never been dogged before.

I've been on a couple of hunts where you park the truck, walk for eight hours, get nothing, and on the way back catch a pig 50 metres from the truck. There's a lot of walking for nothing but it's all part of the fun of it. If you knew exactly what was going to happen every time you went hunting, you'd never bother going. Sometimes I've been on horseback for two days and caught nothing. My brother-in-law has been up in the bush for a week and come back without a pig. The thing that keeps me going is that I know you've got to be in it to win it.

Some of the best hunting trips I've been on were those where I didn't really catch anything. It's about being out there and being in the game. It's about spending time with my mates and my family.

My wife's brother lives down on the East Cape and I love going to visit him. They haven't got as many hunters down there and there are loads of pigs. Being able to go hunting, diving and fishing all in the one day is something I can't do here in the Waikato. He lives out in the middle of nowhere. It's a bit different to where I grew up because they've actually got shops. But it can be pretty hard to predict when they're going to be open so you still have to go looking for your own food! As soon as we get down there, my brother-in-law and I will jump on the horses and be gone for a couple of days. Jerusha isn't so keen on that! She wants to spend time with her brother but as soon as we get there, he and I disappear off hunting.

On one of my favourite hunting trips, I didn't even get the pig myself. I had just had an operation on my leg but I still had to run the dogs. Even though I had stitches in my knee and couldn't move very fast, I took the dogs out into the bush with Jerusha and Leif. My plan had been just to exercise the dogs, but they took off and found themselves a pig. Because of my leg, I couldn't get up to where the dogs were.

I could hear that the dogs were on the pig and they weren't going to let it go. It was really stressing me out so I handed Jerusha the knife and said, 'Go get it!' She took off without hearing any of the instructions I was giving her. She quickly came back so I could tell her how to stick the pig. She looked up to where the dogs were and said to me, 'But there's no track . . .' I said, 'You've just got to make a track.' She took off again, hacking her way through the bush to where the dogs were.

It felt like ages before she got there and all the time I could hear the pig squealing. I was screaming at Jerusha and Leif to hurry up and get to the pig. I hated hearing it make that noise for all that time. Eventually, they got up there, and Jerusha stuck it and killed it. I was so proud of both of them. It was their first time being on a pig and they did really well. Jerusha even carried it out to the truck with the guts still in it. That's not easy given that the guts make up about a third of the weight of a pig.

Before that, Jerusha used to give me a hard time about going out hunting and not catching anything. I think she thought I was out there chasing butterflies! But after that trip she really understood what it is that I do out there. She's been hooked ever since — and that makes it easier for me to go hunting. Sometimes we even take the kids and they love it too. The first time we took our three-year-old, Rome, I thought he'd bawl his eyes out when he saw the dogs attacking the pig, but he was really cool about it. I do try to take them whenever I can because it's a great way for them to learn about where food comes from and I want them to have the same sort of experiences as I did when I was growing up.

The kids are so into it that I recently got called into the local kindy because one of our boys had been busy issuing all the other kids with pig-hunting licences!

The teachers were keen for me to go in and talk to the kids about pig hunting and explain what it was all about. I took a pig in with me for them to have a look at and then gave them all a good feed of wild pork sausages.

I take my pigs to a good local homekill butcher who makes up sausages and bacon for me. They've got so much more flavour than the store-bought stuff. The best time to harvest wild pork is when the pigs have been eating wild berries. The berries sweeten the flavour of the meat. That pork tastes so much sweeter than the stuff you get from pigs that live in the pine forests. In the pines, there's bugger all native berries so the pigs are eating fern shoots, bracken, worms and huhu grubs. If that's what they're eating, that's what they're going to taste like. You're also going to end up with tough pork because the pig's working hard to get his food. Sometimes, with a pig that's come out of the pine forest, you can taste the pine in the meat.

Pigs in the native forest are pretty clever. They know what food's in season and when the berries come on, they'll go straight for them. That's why, when you're a hunter, as soon as the berries are ripe, you go straight to where they are with your dogs because that's where the pigs are going to be. And if the pigs have been eating berries for a while, they will have really packed on the weight because the berries are easy to get and full of sugar. Once the berries are done, the pigs will go and look for another food source.

When we first got together, my wife wouldn't eat wild pork. She'd see me carrying the pig out of the bush and it'd be covered in mud and blood and stuff. She didn't even want to look at it, much less actually eat it. It used to kind of upset me

that I'd gone to all the effort of bringing this massive beast out of the bush on my back and no one would want to eat it. Eventually, I realised that if I took all the hair off the pig, cut it up, cooked it, worked out the flavours and made it look and, more importantly, taste nice, then everyone would forget that it had been a big bloody hairy beast. That became my challenge. Once I managed to find that perfect balance even Jerusha couldn't resist wild pork when I cooked it up.

When you carry an animal out of the bush, you don't want anything to go to waste. It's hard work carrying out 70 kilos of pig on your back.

It might take you an hour to walk in but it can take you nine hours to carry a pig back out again. After all that, by God, you're going to eat every little last bit of it. Whatever we don't eat the dogs get, so nothing's wasted.

PORK & WATER-CRESS PIE

Preheat oven to 200°C.

In a large saucepan, sauté onion and garlic in a little oil until translucent. Add pork, kumara and thyme and cook for 8 minutes. Then add watercress and cook for a further 5 minutes. Season with salt and pepper, sprinkle over flour and stir through. Add chicken stock and bring to the boil, stirring all the time. Then strain, reserving the juices, and place pork mixture in an ovenproof dish.

On a floured bench, roll out flaky pastry to fit dish and place on top of filling, pressing down the edges. Brush pastry with beaten egg.

Bake for 20 minutes or until pastry is golden.

Return reserved cooking juices to a hot frying pan and reduce to a thick gravy.

Serve pie with peas and mashed potatoes and drizzle over gravy.

SERVES 6

1 onion, roughly chopped
1 clove garlic, finely chopped
cooking oil for frying
300g pork strips, roughly chopped
1 large orange kumara,
    roughly chopped
2 sprigs thyme
1 bunch watercress, chopped
salt and pepper
3 tablespoons flour
500ml chicken stock
1 sheet flaky pastry
1 egg, beaten

SPAGHETTI AMATRICIANA

Don't worry if you don't have wild pork bacon handy; smoked streaky bacon works fine.

Place tomatoes, balsamic and brown sugar in a small saucepan and bring to a gentle simmer. When skin on tomatoes start to blister, remove from heat and set aside.

Cook spaghetti in a large saucepan of boiling salted water until al dente (firm to the bite). Strain. Drizzle over olive oil and toss through. Set aside.

Bring a frying pan to a medium-hot heat and brown bacon in a little oil. Then add onion and garlic and cook until just tender. Add a pinch of pepper and toss pasta through. Strain tomatoes and add to the pan, gently tossing through.

Place pasta and sauce on plates, garnish with basil leaves and sprinkle with Parmesan.

SERVES 2

250g cherry tomatoes
250ml balsamic vinegar
2 tablespoons brown sugar
250g dried spaghetti
8 tablespoons olive oil
6 rashers wild pork bacon, roughly chopped
cooking oil for frying
½ red onion, finely sliced
1 clove garlic, finely chopped
pepper
24 basil leaves for garnish
4 tablespoons grated Parmesan for garnish

PORK BELLY WITH CAULIFLOWER PURÉE & BEETROOT & APPLE CHUTNEY

You can press the pork belly before you cook it to get a more uniform piece that will cook more evenly. Cut the pork belly to the size of the roasting dish or find a pan around the same size to cook it in or you could find yourself using litres of oil.

SERVES 4

Pork Belly
500g pork belly
olive oil
salt and pepper
6 whole cloves garlic

Cauliflower Purée
1 head cauliflower, cut into florets
1 onion, chopped
1 clove garlic, chopped
cooking oil for frying
25g butter
50ml cream
salt and pepper

Apple and Beetroot Chutney
See page 167

Preheat oven to 120°C. Line a roasting pan that just fits the pork belly with baking paper.

For the pork belly, score skin in a criss-cross pattern and rub with olive oil and salt and pepper. Place pork belly skin side down in roasting pan. Cover with olive oil and add garlic cloves. Cover with another sheet of baking paper.

Roast for 3 hours then turn oven off and let pork cool in oil. Remove when cold. Place pork belly between two sheets of baking paper and two chopping boards and flatten with a weight of 10–20kg. Place in fridge for 6 hours, then trim edges and cut into four even-sized portions and set aside.

For the purée, cook cauliflower in boiling salted water until tender. Drain and set aside.

Sauté onion and garlic in a little oil in a frying pan over a medium heat, trying not to brown them. Add cauliflower and butter and cream. Blend with a stick blender until smooth. Season to taste with salt and pepper. Set aside, keeping warm.

Preheat oven to 180°C.

Rub more oil, salt and pepper into skin of each portion of pork. Place skin side down in a medium-hot frying pan and fry for about 5 minutes until skin has crisped up. Try not to burn it. Turn over and transfer to oven for 15 minutes. Take out and rest for 5 minutes.

For the chutney, see page 167.

Serve pork with purée, chutney and your favourite greens.

SPAGHETTI CALABRESE

This is another quick and easy Italian recipe that can be enjoyed all year round, and a good way to use up those little ends and bits of salami that never get eaten.

Sauté onion and garlic in a hot frying pan in a little olive oil until translucent. Sprinkle over chilli and cook for 1 minute then add olives and salami and cook for a further 2 minutes.

Pour in pasta sauce, stirring constantly, and season with salt and pepper. Add spaghetti, coating in sauce, and cook until spaghetti is warmed through.

Serve garnished with basil and Parmesan.

SERVES 2

1 small onion, finely sliced
1 clove garlic, finely chopped
olive oil for frying
1 pinch chilli flakes
½ cup Kalamata olives, sliced
100g wild pork salami,
    finely chopped
500ml tomato pasta sauce
salt and pepper
500g cooked spaghetti
basil leaves for garnish
grated Parmesan for garnish,
    if desired

WILD PORK WITH MUSHROOMS & MARSALA

If the sauce is too thin, you can thicken it by sprinkling over a couple of pinches of flour at the reducing stage.

Lightly dust pork medallions in seasoned flour.

Cook medallions in a little olive oil in a frying pan over a medium-hot heat for 1–2 minutes each side until browned nicely. Add mushrooms and onion on top of pork and cook for a few minutes. Pour in marsala and reduce until slightly thickened and pork is cooked right through. Season with salt and pepper.

Serve immediately with steamed vegetables.

SERVES 2

200g wild pork tenderloins, cut into medallions and flattened
½ cup flour, seasoned with salt and pepper
olive oil for frying
½ cup button mushrooms, thinly sliced
1 large onion, finely sliced
½ cup marsala wine
salt and pepper

BOIL-UP

SERVES 4–6

1kg wild pork bones
1 bacon hock
salt
4 medium-sized potatoes,
   peeled and cubed
2 large kumara, peeled and cubed
½ pumpkin, peeled and cubed
4 kamokamo, peeled,
   de-seeded and cubed
1 cup flour
2 teaspoons baking powder
¼ cup water
1 large bunch watercress

This dish has been in my family for as long as
I can remember and is everyone's favourite. It's
even better served with freshly baked Māori bread
or fried bread. (See page 177 for information on
kamokamo.)

Place pork bones and hock in a large stockpot. Pour in just
enough water to cover bones and hock, season with salt
and then gently simmer for 1½ hours. Add potatoes,
kumara, pumpkin and kamokamo to the pot.

Meanwhile, combine flour and baking powder and season
with salt. Gradually add water to form a dough. Break off
small bits of dough and form balls.

Place watercress and doughboys on top of boil-up and
cook until watercress is tender.

Serve hot with Māori bread (see page 180).

BRAWN

SERVES 10

1 pickled wild boar head, skinned
4 pickled beef shins on the bone
4-6 onions, finely diced
3 cloves garlic, finely chopped
2cm knob ginger, grated
1 tablespoon nutmeg
1 tablespoon dried oregano
1 tablespoon dried thyme
salt and pepper

Making brawn with a pickled head and shins gives the dish a better flavour. Ask your local butcher or homekill game butcher to do this for you. You can trim off the snout and ears, too, if you like. This is one of those dishes you can pull out of the fridge and graze on for a week.

Remove eyes from boar's head.

Place shin bones in the bottom of a large stockpot and place boar's head on top. Fill pot with just enough water to cover the head and boil for 4 hours. The meat should be falling off the bones but you may need to scrape off any bits still stuck to them. Take bones out of the pot and with a big wooden spoon roughly break up meat left in the pot.

Add onion, garlic, ginger, nutmeg, oregano, thyme, salt and pepper and boil for 2 hours. Strain through a colander, reserving liquid, and place meat solids into a roasting dish. Spread evenly in the dish and just cover with reserved liquid. Place in the fridge for 6 hours to set.

When ready to eat, cut into squares or smear on toast with a tomato relish. Enjoy!

PORK RACK WITH KUMARA MASH & PORT JUS

SERVES 2

Pork Rack
1 × 8-rib pork rack
cooking oil
salt and pepper

Kumara Mash
1 large orange kumara
25ml cream
50g butter
salt and pepper

Port Jus
50ml chicken stock
50ml Madeira port
15g butter

Preheat oven to 160°C.

For the pork, rub pork rack with oil and season with salt and pepper.

Place rack skin side down in a hot frying pan and cook for 5 minutes. Turn and cook for a further 2 minutes. Transfer to a baking tray.

Cook in oven for 20 minutes. Take out and rest for 10 minutes, keeping warm.

For the mash, cook kumara in boiling salted water until tender. Drain. Return to pot and mash with cream and butter. Season with salt and pepper to taste.

Put the same pan used to cook pork back on the heat and de-glaze with chicken stock, scraping up any excess juices. Reduce by half. Add port and reduce by half again. Then add butter, stirring through until sauce thickens. Keep warm until ready to serve.

Cut pork into cutlets and serve on mash, along with your favourite greens. Drizzle over jus.

WILD PORK WONTON SOUP

A nice, light meal that tastes great. If you don't have wild pork handy, any pork mince will work, or even chicken.

For the wontons, place mince, onion, garlic, ginger, brown sugar and soy sauce in a bowl. Combine well using your hands. Halve the mixture and roll each half into 12 even-sized balls.

Place a wonton wrapper on a floured bench and place a ball of mixture in the middle. Wet edges of wrapper with a little water, fold and pinch edges together to form a wonton. Repeat until all mixture and wrappers are used.

For the broth, pour chicken stock into a large saucepan and bring to the boil. Add ginger, spring onion and soy sauce, and season to taste with salt and pepper. Turn heat down to a gentle simmer and add wontons, cooking for 7–8 minutes or until cooked through. With a few minutes of cooking time left, add carrot.

Serve immediately in bowls and garnish with baby watercress.

SERVES 2–4

Wild Pork Wontons
300g wild boar mince
1 small onion, finely chopped
1 clove garlic, finely chopped
2cm knob ginger, minced
2 tablespoons brown sugar
2 tablespoons dark soy sauce
24 wonton wrappers

Broth
1 litre chicken stock
3cm knob ginger, julienned
1 spring onion, finely sliced
2 tablespoons dark soy sauce
salt and pepper
1 carrot, julienned
1 bunch baby watercress
  for garnish

WILD BOAR BURGERS WITH CAMEMBERT & BALSAMIC ONIONS

SERVES 2

Balsamic Onions
1 large red onion, sliced
10g butter
50ml red wine
50ml balsamic vinegar
2 teaspoons brown sugar

Wild Boar Patties
1 small onion, finely chopped
1 clove garlic, finely chopped
olive oil for frying
300g wild boar mince
¼ cup sage leaves, finely chopped
salt and pepper
1 round camembert

To Assemble
2 burger buns, toasted
2 tablespoons mayo
50g salad greens

Wild pork has to be my favourite of all meats because of its gaminess and strong porky flavour. Try cooking the patties over a grill or charcoal barbecue to add a touch of smokiness.

For the balsamic onions, sauté onion in butter in a frying pan over a medium heat. Then add wine and reduce by half. Add balsamic and reduce by half again. Sprinkle over brown sugar and stir through a knob of butter. Keep warm.

For the patties, sauté onion and garlic in a little olive oil in a medium-hot frying pan until translucent. Cool and set aside.

Combine mince with cooled onion and garlic and sage in a bowl and season well with salt and pepper. Using your hands, roll into four even-sized balls and set aside.

With a ring mould or cookie cutter, press out the middle of the camembert then slice cheese in half through the middle so you have two rounds.

Flatten meatballs into patties. Place a patty on a floured bench, top with a cheese round, and top with another patty. Press down edges to form one patty. Repeat with remaining ingredients.

Place patties in a medium-hot frying pan with oil and cook for 3–4 minutes each side.

Assemble burgers — bun base, mayo, salad greens, patty, balsamic onions, bun top — and serve.

7
DU
&
BII

CK
AME
BDS

My grandfather used to tell us about when he would go hunting for native birds. It's highly illegal to do this now, but back then that was just how our people got their food. It was their way of living. He reckoned some of them were really good eating and I'm pretty sure it would have been because the birds lived on native berries.

Once the birds were trapped, the tradition was to boil them complete with the guts still in. If the birds had been eating berries, then the fruit would still be in their stomachs. When the bird was cooked, the berries would then flavour the meat from the inside out. It was just another way of using nothing extra but enhancing the flavour.

That's the way I learned to cook. For me, it's always been about improving on the natural flavours. When I was on *MasterChef*, everyone else would be grabbing 20 ingredients and I'd only have seven — but I'd win the challenge. I just think about finding the perfect balance, and getting the flavours right.

I don't reckon you need all that fancy stuff if you know how to put the right ingredients together.

The miro berry has to be my favourite one to cook with. It's what the kererū or wood pigeons love to eat. I reckon that's why pigeons were hunted almost to extinction, because the miro made their meat taste so good. The miro berry has only a thin layer of flesh under the skin, and a big pip that's so hard that if you bit into the berry, you'd probably break your teeth on it. It's quite amazing that something with such a small amount of flesh can add such a huge amount of flavour to a dish. Out in the bush, there are heaps of different berries that you can eat — nīkau berries, supplejack berries, tawa berries, blackberries — mind you, you've got to know which ones you can eat or you could get into serious trouble.

I've learnt which berries were OK to eat from the hunters I've been out in the bush with over the years. When you've been out there for a few days and you haven't caught anything, you can get really hungry. When that happens, berries are a good source of food.

Not many people know that it's possible to catch and eat pūkeko. Until recently, I'd never eaten it because my uncles

used to say, 'Oh, you don't want to eat those, boy, they're tough. They've got these stringy, sinewy tendons running through their legs that get caught in your teeth and they're just horrible.' So I'd never really paid any attention to the pūkeko as a food source.

That all changed when I went over to Fantail Lodge near Katikati to cook for the Gamebird Food Festival. Harrie Geraerts, the chef there, showed me how to cook pūkeko. He used pliers to pull out the sinews, then cooked the meat with a Chinese five-spice mix before stuffing it with prunes. The result was absolutely beautiful.

I always thought because pūkeko are scavenger birds that live in swamps that they'd taste like swamp, but it just proves that cooking something the right way can change the way you think about any type of food.

WILD DUCK, ORANGE & WATERCRESS SALAD

Preheat oven to 180°C.

Score skin of duck breast and season with salt and pepper.

In a medium-hot ovenproof frying pan, fry duck skin side down for 3–4 minutes to render out fat. Turn and fry for another 2 minutes. Then transfer to preheated oven for 6–7 minutes until cooked to medium. Take out and rest for 5 minutes. Slice thinly.

Place watercress in a bowl with orange segments.

Whisk together all the dressing ingredients. Drizzle over watercress and orange segments.

Add slices of duck to salad and serve.

SERVES 2

Salad
1 wild duck breast, skin on
salt and pepper
1 bunch baby watercress
2 oranges, cut into segments,
  pith removed

Dressing
3 tablespoons olive oil
1 tablespoon honey
1 tablespoon wholegrain mustard
1 tablespoon white balsamic
  vinegar

DUCK WITH BUBBLE & SQUEAK & PORT JUS

SERVES 2

2 duck breasts, skin on
salt and pepper

Bubble & Squeak
1 red onion, sliced
1 clove garlic, finely chopped
cooking oil for frying
¼ Savoy cabbage, finely chopped
1 sprig thyme
salt and pepper
1 large potato, cooked and cubed
1 cup cooked and cubed pumpkin
15g butter

Port Jus
4 tablespoons chicken stock
4 tablespoons port

Preheat oven to 180°C.

For the duck, score skin of duck breasts and season well with salt and pepper.

Place duck skin side down in a medium-hot ovenproof frying pan and fry for 3–4 minutes. Turn and cook for a further 2 minutes. Transfer to preheated oven and cook for another 6–7 minutes. Take out and rest for 5 minutes.

For the bubble and squeak, in a medium-hot frying pan sauté onion and garlic in a little oil for 1–2 minutes. Add cabbage and thyme, season with salt and pepper and sauté for 2–3 minutes. Add potato, pumpkin and butter and stir till heated through. Set aside.

For the jus, pour chicken stock into the same pan used to cook the duck. Bring to the boil and reduce by half. Then add port and reduce by half again.

Serve duck breasts on bubble and squeak and drizzle over port jus.

CHICKEN BREAST STUFFED WITH SPINACH, CREAM CHEESE & SUNDRIED TOMATOES WITH WHITE WINE REDUCTION

Preheat oven to 180°C.

For the chicken, butterfly breasts by slicing through each breast on the long side almost to the other edge, taking care not to cut it in half. Open breast out and flatten.

Lay a few spinach leaves on top of each breast, followed by 3 sundried tomatoes. Then top with 2 tablespoons of cream cheese and season with salt and pepper. Fold breasts in half.

Lay 3 rashers of bacon on the bench so they overlap, place stuffed breast on top and roll up tightly. Repeat with remaining bacon and stuffed breast.

Brown chicken in a medium-hot ovenproof frying pan with a little olive oil. Transfer to oven for 15 minutes or until cooked through. Cut chicken into 1cm thick slices and set aside.

For the reduction, pour wine into the same pan used to cook chicken. Bring to the boil and reduce by half again. Then add stock and reduce by half again. Stir through butter.

Drizzle chicken with sauce and serve with a rocket salad.

SERVES 2

Stuffed Chicken Breasts
2 chicken breasts
1 handful spinach leaves
6 sundried tomatoes
4 tablespoons cream cheese
salt and pepper
6 rashers bacon
olive oil for frying

White Wine Reduction
100ml dry white wine
100ml chicken stock
10g butter

One of the things I love about going hunting is that it's a really great release from being in the kitchen all the time. It's a place where I go to get away from it all. Especially after *MasterChef*, when I couldn't walk up town without getting recognised. In the supermarket, people will come over and check out what's in my trolley. They'll dig around and see what's in there and I don't even know them! They'll find two-minute noodles and they'll ask, 'What do you do with those?' I'll just say, 'You pour boiling water over them and that's it.' They'll be like, 'Oh no, you must be doing something different with them!' And I'll reply, 'Nope, just read the instructions on the packet.' It's hilarious.

I have never been a person who likes the lime-
light. That was just the way I was brought up.
With my uncles and my cousins, none of us really
say much. Mind you, once they've had a few
beers they'll tell you their life stories. I never in
a million years thought I'd end up getting this
sort of attention.

For five years I'd been telling Jerusha that I wanted a career
change and I really wanted to cook for a living. I looked at
courses but they were expensive, especially as I had to work
to support the family. Then one day, we saw the last episode
of the first series of *MasterChef*.

It was the first time I'd seen the show and I said to Jerusha,
'I could do that.' I didn't really expect her to take me seriously
but she turned around and said, 'Well, apply then.' We sat
down at the computer and submitted my application but I
never seriously thought I'd have a chance.

When I got through to the auditions, I tried to get out of going
through with it so many times. I'd say to my wife, 'I'm not
doing it.' And she'd ring up my mum and then Mum would
ring me and say, 'You're bloody doing it!' I was worried about
work and my dogs, but they convinced me that they'd take
care of all that.

So I went up to Auckland to audition. The first stage was an
interview and I didn't think I'd make it through that stage.
They asked me all these questions. 'Can you make pasta?'
and I'm like, 'No.' 'Can you make cakes?' and I'm like, 'No.'
Then they asked, 'What do you do?', and I said, 'I go out and
get my own ingredients. I go diving and fishing and hunting,
then come home and cook that up.' They put a big red cross
on my page and I thought, That's it . . . I'm off home!

Then I was told to come back and cook for them tomorrow.
So I went back and cooked the venison dish that they
absolutely loved. It was pretty crazy as I was having to deal
with ingredients that I'd never heard of before. I wish I'd had

pikopiko, watercress, native berries and things like that. That's the stuff that I'm used to cooking with. If I'd had those things they'd have seen a bit more than what they did. Those are all ingredients that I grew up knowing where to find and how to cook.

Before I went on the show, I never used to read cookbooks. It was mostly because you'd open them up and every recipe would have so many ingredients. I wouldn't even know what some of the stuff in the recipes was, so I'd just give up. What I wanted was to use ingredients that every person in New Zealand could go and buy quite easily — stuff that you can find in the local Four Square. Add those simple ingredients to food that you can get yourself — hunting, fishing or foraging — and you should have everything you need.

It's also important to me to use ingredients that people can understand. I know that if I was scared off cooking from recipe books then heaps of other people will be too. Those are the people who I want to cook for. Being on *MasterChef*, I was nowhere near as schooled as a lot of the other contestants. I guess it came down to my natural ability, combined with a bit of imagination, combined with the right flavours which worked for me. Some people found it hard when there was one ingredient missing from what they wanted to cook. I was used to cooking with hardly anything and I think it showed.

When we were filming the show, some of the contestants were sitting around talking about restaurants. They asked me what restaurants I went to and I said, 'I haven't been to one for about eight years.' They couldn't believe it. Then someone asked me where I get my inspiration from. I had to explain that I just come up with ideas myself.

When we got into the more complicated dishes in the show, I struggled, especially when we had to cook other cuisines that I hadn't even tasted. When I left the show, I was actually happy to be going home. I'd been away from the family and my dogs for two months. That was the longest I'd ever been away from them and it was a relief when I finally got home.

LAMB'S FRY

SERVES 2

---

1 onion, finely sliced
1 clove garlic, finely chopped
cooking oil for frying
4 rashers bacon, roughly chopped
2 tablespoons flour
salt and pepper
300g lamb's liver, sliced length-
    ways into 3cm thick slivers
12 button mushrooms, halved
150ml mirin
70ml rice wine vinegar
50g butter, chopped

Mirin adds sweetness to this dish and turns plain old liver, which you would usually feed to the dogs underneath the kitchen table, into something unexpected.

Sauté onion and garlic in a medium-hot frying pan with a little oil until translucent. Remove from pan and set aside. In the same pan, brown bacon and set aside with onion and garlic.

Place flour in a bowl and generously season with salt and pepper. Lightly dust liver with flour. Then place liver in a medium-hot frying pan with a little oil and brown all over. You may have to do this in batches. Drain on paper towels and set aside.

In the same pan, brown mushrooms. Then return onion, garlic, bacon and liver, and stir through. Add mirin and reduce by half. Add rice wine vinegar and reduce by half again. Throw in butter and stir through.

Serve on toast.

LAMB RACK WITH PURPLE POTATO & PIKOPIKO SALAD

SERVES 2

Lamb Rack
1 × 8-rib lamb rack, trimmed
oil
salt
2 tablespoons horopito seasoning

Purple Potato & Pikopiko Salad
8 small purple potatoes, washed
12 slender pikopiko or
    asparagus shoots
salt and pepper
50ml olive oil
3 vine-ripened Campari
    tomatoes, quartered
1 red onion, finely sliced
1 cup baby watercress
30ml balsamic vinegar

Red Wine Reduction
100ml red wine
50ml balsamic vinegar
20g butter

Lamb racks are always great, and this fresh salad makes it a dish to impress the guests. The horopito seasoning, made from the dried leaves of a native plant, adds a peppery earthiness. It can be found in specialist food stores. If you can't find pikopiko, use asparagus instead. You can swap the red wine reduction for any of the other sauces in the sauce section (see pages 168–173).

Preheat oven to 180°C.

For the lamb, rub lamb rack with oil, salt and half the horopito seasoning. Place in a hot frying pan and sear for 2 minutes each side. Pop into oven for 10–12 minutes. Take out and rest for 10 minutes. Slice into cutlets.

For the salad, cook potatoes in boiling salted water until tender. Plunge into chilled water to stop any further cooking.

Blanch pikopiko in boiling water for 2 minutes. Also plunge into chilled water to stop cooking.

Cut potatoes into quarters and place in a bowl with pikopiko, remaining horopito seasoning, a pinch of salt and pepper and olive oil. Stir to combine. Add tomatoes, red onion and watercress. Spoon over balsamic and toss through.

For the reduction, in same pan used to cook the lamb, pour in red wine and reduce by half. Add balsamic and reduce by half again. Then add butter and stir through until thickened.

Arrange salad on plates with lamb on top and drizzle over reduction.

LAMB BACK STRAP WITH PARSNIP PURÉE & RED WINE REDUCTION

New Zealand spring lamb is some of the best meat
I've ever eaten — tender, with just the right amount
of fat. It is beautiful served with parsnip purée
and fresh asparagus, and the red wine reduction
brings it all together.

For the purée, place onion and garlic in a frying pan over
a medium heat and sauté in a little oil without letting them
colour. Add parsnips and milk and simmer until tender.
Drain off any milk then add cream and butter. Transfer to a
blender and blend to a smooth purée. Season to taste with
salt and white pepper. Set aside and keep warm.

Preheat oven to 180°C.

For the lamb, season lamb back strap with salt and pepper.
In a hot ovenproof frying pan sear lamb for 2 minutes on
each side in a little oil and butter. Transfer to oven for
10–12 minutes. Take out and rest for 10 minutes. Slice into
medallions.

For the reduction, in the same pan used to cook the lamb,
pour in wine and reduce by half. Add balsamic and reduce
by half again. Sprinkle over sugar and add butter, stirring
through until thickened.

Drop asparagus into boiling salted water and blanch for
1–2 minutes. Then place in a bowl of cold water to stop
further cooking.

Serve lamb rack with parsnip purée and asparagus,
and drizzle over reduction.

SERVES 2

Parsnip Purée
1 onion, roughly chopped
1 clove garlic, roughly chopped
olive oil for frying
4 parsnips, peeled, cored
   and chopped
1½ cups milk
100ml cream
25g butter
salt and white pepper

Lamb Back Strap
500g lamb back strap, trimmed
salt and black pepper
oil and butter for frying

Red Wine Reduction
150ml red wine
50ml balsamic vinegar
1 tablespoon brown sugar
25g butter

12 asparagus spears

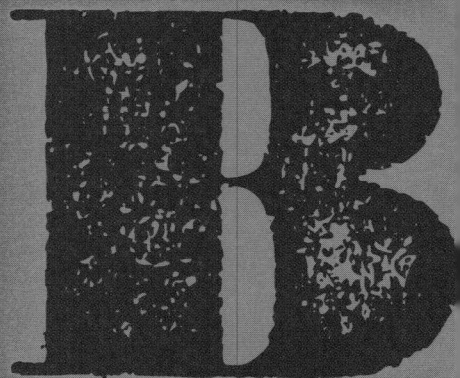

BEEF

9

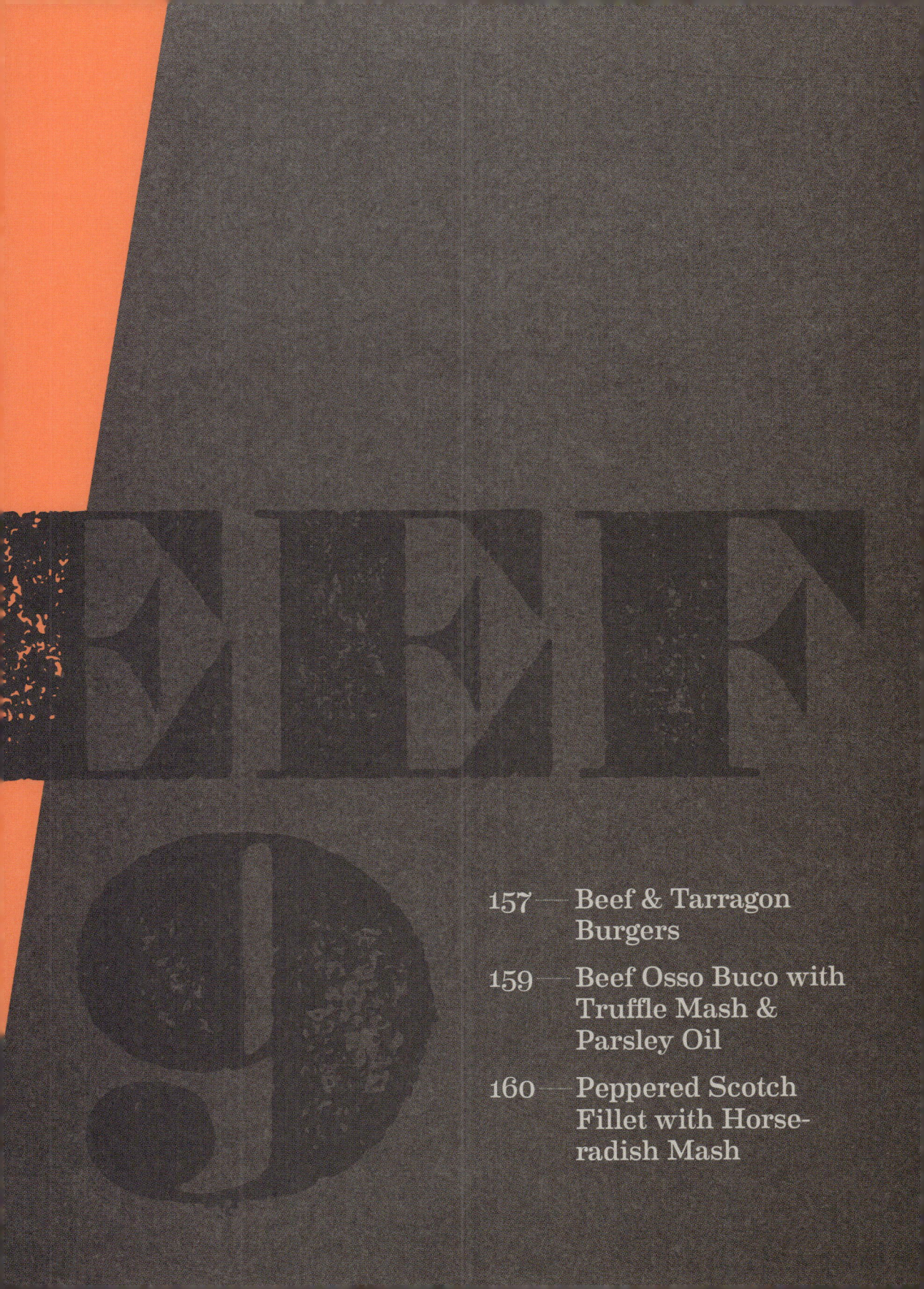

After *MasterChef*, I got a call from Alberico De Andrea, the Italian guy who'd inspired me to want to cook all those years ago. He was still running the restaurant in Tokoroa and he asked me if I wanted to work with him for the Monteith's Wild Food Festival. I was really busy after *MasterChef* doing a lot of interviews and I couldn't do the festival. But I told him that if he had a job coming up in the near future, I'd be keen.

He called me about a month later and offered me a job as an assistant chef. At that stage, I was still working at the chicken farm and I kept doing that while I worked nights at the restaurant.

I love Italian food — Italians are the masters of enhancing natural flavours and working with very little, so their way of eating fits with my food philosophy really well. It was my first job in a professional kitchen and in the four months I worked there, I learnt a hell of a lot.

When Alberico shut the restaurant and went back to Italy for seven weeks, I continued working at the chicken farm. Then one day I got a call offering me a job as head chef at a new restaurant in the Putaruru Heritage Hotel. I thought that was pretty cool until about two weeks before the restaurant opened. Then I started to get really cold feet and wonder what I'd done. I told my wife I wasn't sure about running my own kitchen and she told me I'd be fine. On the first night as chef at The Master's Table, I was a bit scared of jumping into such a huge role but it went really well. And we've continued to do well since. People seem to love my menus so that's been really good.

After working at the chicken factory, I got really sick of seeing chickens. Chicken wouldn't be the first thing I cook for myself but I cook it for the rest of the family. I was the same after I had been working at the meat works.

We were killing sheep every day and that turned me off mutton and lamb for years — although it was where I met my wife Jerusha, so it wasn't all bad!

Once I stopped working at the meat works, I got the hunger back for eating mutton and lamb. I've also worked at a beef plant.

I think having done those jobs has given me a real appreciation for the meat. I can look at the grain and know

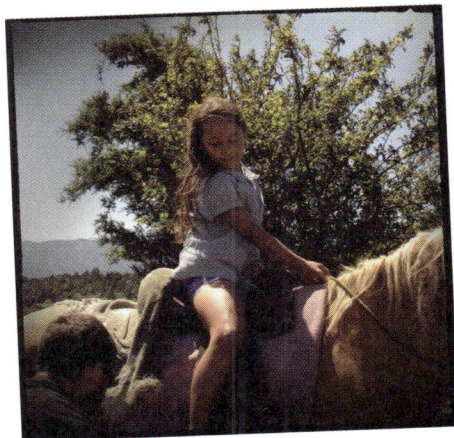

what cooking method is going to suit the meat the best. It also means that I know what part of the beast every cut of meat has come from. I can see the meat as part of a whole animal.

There's no wastage when it comes to Māori cooking. We eat every part of the animal. A lot of people don't like offal but we'll eat the whole lot. One of the dishes I love is terotero, which is sheep's intestines. The first time I had terotero, my brother-in-law cooked it. He just slapped it on a plate and I was like, 'Oooohh, what's that?' And he said, 'Don't ask questions. Just eat it!' I was game to try anything so I bit into it. It wasn't what I expected. It tasted a lot meatier than I thought. A lot of people wouldn't like that. To make terotero, you just boil the intestines for about three hours. It's not the most appealing-looking dish but flavourwise, I reckon it's beautiful.

BEEF & TARRAGON BURGERS

For me, beef, tarragon and mushrooms are a classic combination, making this burger a must-try.

Preheat oven to 180°C.

For the patties, in a hot frying pan sauté onion and garlic in a little oil until translucent. Set aside and cool.

Place mince, cooled onion and garlic, egg, mustard and tarragon in a bowl. Season with salt and pepper. Combine all ingredients with your hands. Roll mixture into two even-sized balls. Flatten into two patties.

Brown patties in a hot ovenproof frying pan with a little oil, cooking for 1 minute each side. Transfer to preheated oven and cook for a further 6 minutes.

For the mayo, combine horseradish and mayo.

Pan-fry mushrooms in a little butter.

Assemble burgers: bun base, salad greens and red onion. Generously drizzle over horseradish mayo and top with a patty, a mushroom, sliced tomato and ketchup. Finish with bun top.

Serve with crunchy fries.

SERVES 2

Beef & Tarragon Patties
1 onion, finely chopped
1 clove garlic, finely chopped
cooking oil for frying
300g beef mince
1 egg
1 tablespoon Dijon mustard
¼ cup fresh tarragon, finely chopped
salt and pepper

Horseradish Mayo
1 tablespoon horseradish
3 tablespoons mayo

To Assemble
2 portobello mushrooms, peeled
butter
2 gourmet burger buns, toasted
2 handfuls salad greens
½ red onion, finely sliced
1 beefsteak tomato, sliced
2 tablespoons ketchup

BEEF OSSO BUCO WITH TRUFFLE MASH & PARSLEY OIL

I first tried this dish at an Italian restaurant I used to work in. The tender melt-in-your-mouth meat together with the sauce it was cooked in was to die for, so I've come up with my own take on osso buco. For a creamier, smoother mash, pass it through a ricer.

Preheat oven to 160°C.

For the osso buco, dust beef shanks with seasoned flour. Brown in a little oil in a cast-iron ovenproof frying pan or flameproof casserole for 2 minutes each side. Remove from pan and set aside.

Place onion, garlic, carrot, celery, bay leaf and thyme in a pan and cook until just soft. Add stock, wine and tomatoes, return meat to pan and bring to the boil. If using a frying pan, transfer mixture to a large ovenproof dish. Cover with lid.

Transfer to oven and cook for 2–2½ hours. Stir through parsley before serving.

For the truffle mash, cook potatoes in boiling water until tender. Drain and return to saucepan and mash with butter and cream. Then add truffle oil, season with salt and pepper and combine. Set aside.

For the parsley oil, place chopped parsley, olive oil and lemon juice and zest in a bowl. Season to taste with salt and pepper and combine well.

Place mash on plates and top with osso buco. Drizzle over parsley oil.

SERVES 2

Beef Osso Buco
2 beef shanks, bone in
4 tablespoons flour, seasoned
  with salt and pepper
cooking oil for frying
1 large onion, finely chopped
2 cloves garlic
1 carrot, cubed
1 stalk of celery, cubed
1 bay leaf
2 sprigs thyme
800ml beef stock
200ml red wine
1 × 420g can chopped tomatoes
¼ cup chopped parsley

Truffle Mash
4 potatoes, peeled and chopped
25g butter
50ml cream
1 tablespoon truffle oil
salt and pepper

Parsley Oil
¼ cup chopped parsley
50ml olive oil
juice and zest of 1 lemon
salt and pepper

PEPPERED SCOTCH FILLET WITH HORSE-RADISH MASH

SERVES 2

Peppered Scotch Fillet
2 × 200g Scotch fillet steaks
¼ cup black peppercorns,
 freshly ground
olive oil for frying

Horseradish Mash
2 large potatoes,
 peeled and chopped
50g butter
20ml cream
salt and pepper
2 tablespoons horseradish
2 tablespoons wholegrain mustard

Red Wine Jus
100ml red wine
100ml beef stock
10g butter

2 large portobello mushrooms,
 peeled and sliced
butter
4 broccoli florets

If you love steak as much as I do then you'll love this dish. It's the horseradish and mustard that changes those boring old spuds into something out of the ordinary.

Preheat oven to 200°C. Line an oven tray with baking paper.

For the Scotch fillet, season steaks generously with freshly ground peppercorns. Shake off any excess pepper.

In a hot frying pan sear steaks in a little olive oil for 1–2 minutes on each side. Transfer to lined oven tray and place in oven for 6 minutes. Take out and rest for 5 minutes.

For the mash, boil potatoes in salted water until tender. Drain and return to pan. Add butter and cream and mash well. Season with salt and pepper, add horseradish and mustard and combine well.

For the jus, in the same pan used to cook the steak, pour in wine and de-glaze pan. Bring to the boil and reduce by half. Add stock and reduce by half again. Stir through butter. Set aside.

Pan-fry mushrooms in a little butter until golden brown.

Steam broccoli until tender.

Serve steak on mash, topped with mushrooms. Pour over jus and serve steamed broccoli on the side.

10
EXTRA
SAUCE

RAS
SETC.

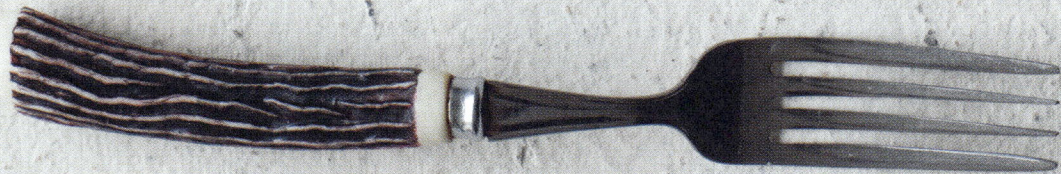

I got a call one day from a producer of the TVNZ show, *Close Up*. He said to me, 'Do you want to make some TV with us in a couple of days' time?' I said, 'Nah, I'm pretty busy at the moment, I don't really have time to do it.' Then he said, 'It'd be spending the day with Rick Stein.' I was like, 'I'll be there!' So two days later, I drove over to Port Waikato and spent the day with Rick. I could barely believe my luck. It's got to be every cook's dream to spend a day with such an amazing chef. I used to watch him on TV all the time — I never would have thought that one day I'd get to meet him, let alone cook with him.

He was such a nice guy — exactly like he is on TV. I was quite nervous but he just came up and introduced himself. Even though I was a bit star-struck, he made me feel really comfortable. He wasn't dressed for the occasion — he had these nice shoes which ended up with cowshit all up the side of them. But he didn't seem to mind.

We had a really full-on schedule for a single day. To start with we went whitebaiting — it was pretty amazing that my first time ever whitebaiting was with Rick Stein!

Mind you, it was his first time too, so I didn't have to worry about him thinking that I didn't know what I was doing. We missed the tide but we still managed to get enough bait for a feed.

Then we went eeling. That was awesome. I love that you can go eeling with different guys — whether it's my mates or someone like Rick — and you always learn something. He told me that the eels migrate every couple of years to Tonga. I'd never heard that before. He didn't mind getting his hands dirty. He was happy getting in and grabbing an eel.

Rick was here promoting Malaysian cooking so he cooked the eel in a Malaysian-style stir-fry. It was really good. He said New Zealand eel was the best he'd ever eaten. I reckon that's because of the purity of our water.

After eeling, it was time to go dragging for flounder. Once we'd caught a few fish, I had to cook them for him. You can bet I was a bit nervous.

It's not every day you get to cook fresh seafood for one of the world's best-known seafood chefs!

As if being nervous wasn't bad enough, I had to cook the flounder on a hotplate outdoors. It was pretty hard to control the heat on it and I ended up burning the fish. Thankfully, Rick didn't seem to mind and ate it anyway.

The only disappointment for me that day was that we were also meant to go pig hunting but we ran out of time. That would have been awesome but maybe we'll get the chance next time he's in town!

BEET- ROOT & APPLE CHUTNEY

MAKES 375g

200ml malt vinegar
½ cup sugar
1 small onion, finely sliced
1 Granny Smith apple, skin on,
    grated
1 × 450g baby beetroot, grated
2 tablespoons horseradish
salt and pepper

Place vinegar and sugar in a saucepan over a medium heat to dissolve sugar. Add onion, apple and beets. Continue stirring until liquid reduces, then add horseradish and season with salt and pepper. Cool.

Serve cold as a condiment for fish and cold meats. This will keep in the fridge for a few weeks.

BLUE-BERRY & GIN GLAZE

MAKES 8 SERVES

1 cup gin
½ cup blueberries
2 tablespoons white sugar

Pour gin into a frying pan over a high heat. Tilt pan towards the heat to ignite the alcohol or light with a match. Once alight, add blueberries and sugar and reduce by half.

Serve over chicken.

RASP-BERRY SAUCE

MAKES 4 SERVES

4 tablespoons raspberry jam
250ml sherry vinegar
15g butter

Place jam and vinegar in a saucepan over a medium heat and bring to a simmer. Strain mixture through a sieve to remove any seeds, then return to the pan and continue to reduce until slightly thickened. Add butter and stir through.

Serve on your favourite cut of wild game.

RED WINE REDUC- TION

MAKES 4 SERVES

½ cup red wine
¼ cup balsamic vinegar
2 tablespoons brown sugar
10g butter

Place red wine in a saucepan over a medium heat and reduce by half to a syrup. Add balsamic and reduce by half again. Sprinkle with brown sugar and stir through butter. Reduce until slightly thick.

Serve over meat or fish.

BLACK-BERRY SAUCE

MAKES 4 SERVES

3 tablespoons blackberry jam
200ml red wine vinegar
10g butter
¼ cup blackberries

Place jam and vinegar in a saucepan over a medium heat. Bring to a simmer, then pass through a sieve to remove any seeds. Return to heat and reduce by half. Add butter and stir through, continuing to reduce until slightly thickened. Add berries and gently stir through.

Serve over venison.

GAME STOCK

MAKES 2 LITRES

2kg venison bones, chopped
cooking oil for frying
2 carrots, roughly chopped
2 onions, roughly chopped
2 stalks celery, roughly chopped

Fry bones in large stockpot with a little oil until nice and brown. Remove from pot and set aside.

Add vegetables to the same pot and again brown nicely. Return bones to pot and cover with water. Bring to the boil then reduce to a simmer. Simmer for 3 hours, skimming off fat when necessary.

Strain through a sieve.

This will keep in the fridge for a few days or freeze until required.

GAME JUS

MAKES APPROX. 1 LITRE

2 litres game stock (see opposite)
2 sprigs thyme
2 bay leaves
250ml red wine
6 peppercorns

Place all ingredients in a large stockpot and reduce by half.

This will keep in the fridge for a few weeks or freeze until required.

Serve over wild game.

GATHERING WATERCRESS, PIKOPIKO & KAMOKAMO

The Māori way is for knowledge to be handed down through the generations. When there was a celebration or a tangi at the marae, the older guys would go hunting and the younger ones would go out and get the watercress, pūhā, eels and trout needed to feed everyone. As you got older, you'd get taught new skills and then, in turn, you'd be expected to pass on those skills to the younger ones. That way there was always enough food and the knowledge of how to find it was passed along. My mum and my uncles were taught by their parents and grandparents; they then handed the knowledge to us.

I will pass that knowledge down to my children and I hope that they will do the same.

One of the people I learned a lot from was my Uncle Louie. I was about five or six when he took me down to the stream and taught me how to pick watercress. He showed me the best stuff to grab and made sure I knew not to pick it if it was flowering as it would be bitter. When it came to getting plants, Uncle Louie saw to it that we all knew what was okay to eat and what could make us sick. He taught us properly

and watched what we picked. Once he was satisfied that we knew what we were doing, he was quite happy to send us out to get watercress and he knew he wouldn't have to worry about us.

Just like there's hundreds of different types of ferns, there's hundreds of different types of pikopiko. The more I go out into the bush with different people and in different places, the more types of pikopiko I discover. It's important you know what you're picking though, as some fern shoots aren't safe to eat. While there are some pikopiko that are about the size of asparagus, they can be a bit woody. I much prefer the small, tender shoots. They might only be a couple of centimetres long but they're really sweet and tasty.

Kamokamo is a type of squash. When I was growing up, there was a family who used to have a huge garden and they would drive around selling their produce off the back of their truck.

Their kamokamo was absolutely beautiful. I love them just boiled in water until they're a bit soft then served with a bit of salt and butter. Simple but delicious.

The kamokamo flowers are good to eat too. They're just like zucchini flowers. We used to mix them up with pūhā and watercress and put them into the boil-up.

The best time to eat kamokamo is when it's still small enough to fit in your hand. When it's like that the seeds are still soft and you can swallow them easily. If it gets too big, the seeds go hard and it's a pain to spit them out. It's better if you keep the big ones and dry out the seeds for planting next season — especially if it's been a good crop. Good seeds will almost guarantee the quality of the next season's crop.

FRIED BREAD

Place sugar and yeast in a bowl. Add water and mix to dissolve and activate yeast. Add flour a bit at a time and combine well until a dough forms. Leave to rise in a warm place for about 30 minutes, then take out and knead until just firm.

Flatten dough and cut into pieces.

Place dough pieces in a hot frying pan and fry in oil for 2–3 minutes each side or until golden brown.

Serve hot with golden syrup or jam, or as a side to hot soups or stews.

MAKES 12 PIECES

1 teaspoon sugar
1 tablespoon yeast
2 cups lukewarm water
3 cups flour
cooking oil for frying

MĀORI BREAD

If you have the time you can punch down and rise the bread several times for a denser loaf.

For the batter, put flour and yeast into a bowl with warm water and leave for 10–20 minutes to rise and bubble.

For the dough, place second measure of flour in a bowl and make a well in the middle. Pour in batter and second measure of water, along with sugar and salt. Mix to form a dough and knead until smooth and elastic. Put dough into a buttered pot and leave to rise in a warm place until doubled in size.

Preheat oven to 180°C.

Bake bread for 1 hour. You will know when your bread is done by the smell and it will sound hollow when you tap it.

Turn out and wrap in a damp cloth to keep fresh.

Serve with venison casserole and boil-up (see pages 25 and 117) or with stews.

MAKES 1 LOAF

Batter
2 cups flour
2 tablespoons yeast
  (I use Surebake)
1 cup warm water

Dough
8 cups flour
3 cups water
3 tablespoons sugar
1 teaspoon salt

ACK-NOW-LEDGE-MENTS

There are a few people I would like to thank. My wife, Jerusha, for pushing me to apply for *MasterChef* and follow my passion for food, and for being there for the kids when I couldn't be. Thanks for holding down the fort when I'm away — you're a soldier and I love ya, hun.

My mum and dad for supporting me through the years, for teaching me the values of good food as a child, for helping me develop my passion and always pushing me to better myself but, most of all, keeping me grounded throughout this whole experience.

My sous chef, Nathan Arnell, for helping me with the preparation for this book.

Kieran Scott for the awesome photography — you are the man.

Imagination Television for giving the ole Maori boy from Putaruru a crack in the spotlight. It has been a life-changing experience that I will never forget.

My fellow masterchefs who I met along the way — Jax, Nadia, Stu, Michelle, ninja Michael, Kathleen, Sam, Fiona, Rob, Anthony, Traceylee and Dan the man. I'll never forget the time we shared in the house and couldn't have picked a better bunch of people to take the journey with.

Special thanks to Nicola McCloy for her help with the stories.

Random House for giving me the opportunity to write my first book. It has been a pleasure working with you.

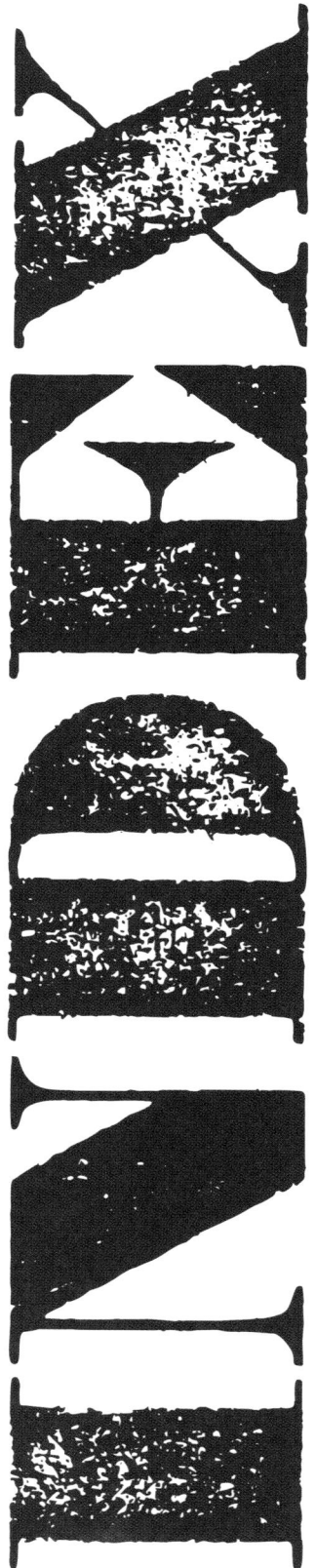

INDEX

V

W